Making Sense of What Hasn't Made Sense

Making Sense of What Hasn't Made Sense

DR. RAMONA ROBERTS

MAKING SENSE OF WHAT HASN'T MADE SENSE

iUniverse books may be ordered through booksellers or by contacting:

iUniverse
1663 Liberty Drive
Bloomington, IN 47403
www.iuniverse.com
844-349-9409

Because of the dynamic nature of the Internet, any web addresses or links contained in this book may have changed since publication and may no longer be valid. The views expressed in this work are solely those of the author and do not necessarily reflect the views of the publisher, and the publisher hereby disclaims any responsibility for them.

Any people depicted in stock imagery provided by Getty Images are models, and such images are being used for illustrative purposes only.
Certain stock imagery © Getty Images.

ISBN: 978-1-6632-4175-7 (sc)
ISBN: 978-1-6632-4176-4 (e)

Library of Congress Control Number: 2022912110

Print information available on the last page.

iUniverse rev. date: 06/30/2022

Contents

About The Covers

A caterpillar's transformation may be fantastic to watch on the outside, yet it can get grisly deep inside the chrysalis with the digestion process and growth of the body parts. The chrysalis is a time of drawing inward with reflection, maybe over-analysis and confusion. Some may get lucky to see the butterfly formed inside the chrysalis yet stay away from the temptation to help cut it open to let it out. Its wings need just the right time in there to fully form; it must go through pain and struggle to emerge ready to take flight. The butterfly doesn't look back at its caterpillar self with any judgment, it simply flies on. And we can pause for a moment when we see it in all its beauty, to reflect on our own metamorphosis and know that our pain and struggle do not have to be futile.

The front and back cover paintings can be viewed/purchased in original or print form along with the rest of Joe Palmerio's (my pop) butterfly series and other artwork at http://palmerioart.com/.

Front cover selection: Chrysalis
Back cover selection: Feeding Time

Introduction

Throughout the years of my son's life, I somehow managed to escape all the Marvel movies while he and my husband made it to every single one. I did keep up with his interests in the toys, but it was a month before he was turning sixteen that I made a conscious effort and commitment to him to take on a Marvel movie marathon. This is the challenge when our children become teenagers, to lean into their interests and their world a bit, and surprisingly I was hooked and feeling like I could not wait until the next weekend to see what happens in the next one. In *Endgame* (2019) I heard Bruce Banner speak about "for years I've been treating the Hulk like he's some kind of disease, something to get rid of" and how he combined the brains and the brawn to be the best of both worlds. It struck me because I have been using Hulk as a reference for many years and have had clients use the reference themselves unsolicited.

Countless clients have shared examples of behaviors and responses that seem out of their character, and they express confusion and question of why they have acted in such a way. Family members and friends have called them all kinds of names and urge question of their sanity. A past client of mine used the reference when referring to a recent verbal blowup she had with her partner as a "Hulk-Rage" event. Although in the films the behavior is much more rage and aggression based, I think clinically we can alter this inner part to capture all types of responses that come from a place of fear, mistrust, and feeling triggered.

I had a bit of an "oh my goodness" reaction as I heard Bruce in the film speak about his struggle with this part of himself. Hearing him speak about the merging of his parts connected in my mind to therapy. I also enjoyed Pixar's *Turning Red* (2022) that show-cased Mei's inner red panda, albeit its representation is tied to puberty and growing up, the way Mei integrates what is happening internally lends itself to a lot of internal part-focused work that takes place in the trauma field. Self-compassion has been my schtick for so long in my work with survivors of trauma and it is incorporated into several treatment modalities already established.

I wanted to provide material to reach a need that I started to pay attention to in my clinical work. Emails would come in asking for a quick read to help family members being able to wrap their head around a trauma diagnosis of a loved one. Oftentimes it was being identified in a time of crisis and I did not want to offer up lengthy recommendations to start off with. And I would not even be able to count how many patients would go through their treatment, groups, individual sessions, and share midway and at the time of discharge how much they wished their partners, parents, adult children, and others need to learn the stuff that they are getting educated in that is specifically related to trauma. Many commented that it would help their relationships by the other person recognizing what is behind their behavior to help them not take it personally as well as to potentially alter the typical response elicited in their loved one. So, I took the request and created a webinar that was presented with a few colleagues. Then I realized I could spread the knowledge around a bit more if I put pen to paper like this.

Maybe you picked this book up to help you understand your own individual experiences better, to wrap your mind around a loved one's diagnosis, or maybe you are a student or beginning clinician looking to improve your conceptualization of how trauma impacts your clients/patients. There are trainings and books that you can find authored from a range of experts to survivors themselves. This book is intended to provide you with a snapshot review of how to think about trauma and the way you define it, as well as the impact of trauma in several areas impacting a survivor, in how it distorts perception and cognition; drives behavior; clouds one's sense of safety, power, and control; and leaves one void of true intimacy. My hope is that upon completion of its content, it will at minimum help you gain an awareness and appreciation for the impact of trauma, which to me is foundational to being able to provide the support that the survivor needs. It is my aim that reading this helps you start to make sense of what hasn't made sense for so long.

My next level goal is to bring about a sense of compassion and depending on the reader, that may be self-directed. And going one step further, it may be to encourage someone to start or continue their journey of finding their ideal version of self now that they have some pieces of the puzzle that may have been missing. This may be just enough to start you on path of understanding and propel you into further reading and/or treatment either for your own experience of healing from trauma or to be supportive of your experience with a loved one.

SECTION 1

Childhood Development 101

To understand the impact of trauma I believe it is important to take a step back and understand a little bit of child development that helps us grasp the foundation that is laid for our minds and bodies to respond to trauma as some do. As the diverse types are presented in a later section, you will also see how experiences with trauma undergone early in life may itself impede the expected development with longer term implications.

Understanding early cognitive experiences and development

For our purposes, we will be working from the term cognition as referring to the way in which we process information; acquire knowledge; learn, store, and retrieve material; and the way we think about events and experiences. It has to do with our perception which in turn influences our reactions. Jean Piaget, a psychologist best known for his research on children's cognitive development, believed that children pass through a series of stages in developing intelligence and formal thought processes. His constructivism theory suggests that individuals actively construct higher level of knowledge from biological maturation and the environment. And revolutionary changes in thought occur at a few different points in childhood (believed to be around the ages of two, six-seven, and eleven). Like mini researchers, they are adapting to and learning their environment.

Children are like little scientists constantly trying to make sense of their world by testing out their own theories. They are active learners or experimenters and are intrinsically motivated to seek out and understand new information that is presented to them (Broderick & Brewitt, 2020). They actively experiment in infancy with dropping and shaking objects just to see what happens. If you are a caregiver, sibling, parent, or childcare worker this may bring up some funny images.

With this perspective, one can be entertained by a young child's actions as I think of a classic example of a parent and child with a stroller or cart in a store. You may have experienced it firsthand or witnessed this interaction when a child throws a toy, and it lands on the floor. What may happen next is the parent returns the toy to the child and quickly it is found back on the floor. This exchange may go on a few times until the parent's frustration tolerance gets the best of them and they put the toy away and out of reach for the child. The parent may see this behavior as not listening or obeying but picture this baby and what may be going on in their minds as a little scientist. I imagine the self-talk goes a bit like this "Hey neat, I threw something, and my dad picked it up and it is back in my lap. Let me see what happens if I throw it again. Wow, check that out, I did something that got him to do something in return- is this that thing called cause and effect? Am I creating some sort of pattern? Oh man! just when I discovered something my dad stopped all the fun."

We are taught that children develop and see the world through what we refer to as a schema, which is information grouped together that is learned through their experiences and interactions. And we have several different schemata that get created. In psychology we often refer to them as psychological structures that help organize our experience and guide our thoughts and behaviors. "By adulthood we have built countless schemas, ranging from cats and dogs to our concept of love (Myers, 2014, p.125)." During infancy, most are based on actions for example "objects that can be sucked." Later, they are based on functional or conceptual relationships like "things I use to eat with." As children move into adolescence this progresses to abstract properties.

There is a process of adaptation, or an adjustment to change, that takes place as the child's understandings are gradually shifted and modified as they interact with their environment. A couple aspects of adaptation are terms known as assimilation and accommodation and you will see these come back around later in this book to help you understand the cognitive impact of trauma. But first, to understand these in general terms, assimilation is incorporating new ideas into existing schemata. This is when the child will extend an existing schema to new objects or situations. An example is when a child learns that their four-legged pet is called a dog and then every deer that runs across the road or cow they may see on a road trip is referred to as a dog. They are taking in that sensory information from what they see and are joining it with the existing schema they have formed that four-legged animals are called dog. At some point, someone accompanying them corrects them and says, "that is a different animal, your pet is a dog but that is a cow." The child now must modify their existing schema based on their new experiences, which is known as accommodation, to understand that not all four-legged animals are referred to as a dog.

Remember, as little scientists they are continually testing out their theories, and when their theory does not test out successfully, they must change it. When they go to grab an object, they may learn "oh, heavy objects take two hands" and then that shifts the theory about how to handle objects. This is like errors noted in language development of what is referred to as underextension and overextension. The former is displayed in a child applying a word too narrowly to a situation or an object, like the child who insists that a "bowl" is what they use for cereal and cannot possibly be what you may use to eat your oatmeal or spaghetti; it has one role. The latter is when they apply the word to a wider collection of objects or events where it may not be applicable. This may be using the term "bowl" to describe anything you eat from in your kitchen.

Another interesting piece that is developed early on in childhood, between four and eight months that has later implications in our decision making, is that of intention. As early as three and four months of age we are seeing babies make connections in causality and by about eight months, they have what is referred to as deliberate/intentional behavior or means-to an-end behavior where they see themselves as not having to be resigned to sitting and waiting patiently for things to happen, or solely relying on reflexes; they can initiate action and move something that is in the way of their toy. Eight months is a busy time with acquiring knowledge and ability and brings on the understanding that objects exist independently. Prior to this, you may recall trying to hide a toy from a baby and notice that early on, they think it is gone and become quite amused when it resurfaces. If you have played the game of peek-a-boo with an infant, they think it is the greatest magician act of all time and can keep them giggling for hours.

After developing this object permanence, now a child will actively look for the toy that is hidden; it is no longer out of sight, out of mind. It involves representational thought where they can think about something that is not currently stimulating their senses at that moment. Object constancy follows this and has more to do with the way we look at interpersonal relationships and our ability to bounce back after experiencing some setback, conflict, or ambiguity in a relationship. This is first influenced by the relationship with the child and caregiver. Intersensory integration also comes into play where the child perceives an object in one way (sees a bumpy surface of a teething toy) and constructs an idea of its other perceptual characteristics. These are like built in short cuts for us to keep us working efficiently (spoiler alert, short cuts don't always work out well in how our brains perceive and interpret our world).

The behavior sequences obviously become more complex with each month that passes and by age two they can engage in some problem solving mentally. Intentionally controlling our own behavior and thought in terms of planning, judgment, decision making, setting goals, choosing what we pay attention to, and deciding to make one response over another, are all cognitive processes that we refer to as executive functioning. These are governed by the prefrontal cortex (picture behind your forehead and you will learn more in a later section) which can show maturational gains later in the first year of life and are accepted in the field as not being fully formed until someone's early to mid-20s. You will start to notice that we can incorrectly make connections between these concepts of cause-and-effect and intentional behavior, and we can make meaning out of things that do not actually exist. Anyone of us right now in a rational thinking state can see that we may have control over some things but not all. I cannot control the weather, but I can have some decision-making power in looking at the daily weather report, pack an umbrella, and wear rain boots. How soon we can forget this concept when we have experiences that bring in the unwarranted self-blame and guilt that we'll get into soon.

But what about inferring others' intent? Referred to as a theory of mind, is the ability to infer another's representational state and to predict behavior accordingly. The biggest shifts in this ability occur between two-three, four-five, and after five years old. Between the ages of two-three a child begins to take in the idea of others' mental states maybe being different than theirs and that we all vary in our perceptions, emotions, and desires that influence our behavior. From four-five they are now starting to understand that another person's thoughts may be false or inaccurate and they may act on them. After the age of five, there is a realization that other peoples' actions are not always consistent with their true thoughts and feelings and that people interpret events differently.

There is a term, egocentrism, which describes children struggling to understand another's outlook, or that others differ in ideas, emotions, thoughts, and perceptions. The child initially believes that others see the world as they do. Think about a time when a child was speaking about something in their visual field (their view), and you cannot see it based on where you are positioned. The child does not understand that you cannot see the same thing as them, until they get a little older and progress cognitively. This also may help explain when your 4-year-old thinks you want Playdoh for your 42nd birthday too, obviously because they want it and who could ever resist Playdoh!? I mean c'mon, how is that not the best gift ever. Or a scenario where you are playing cards or a board game with a 6-year-old and he calls you mean for winning because his desire to win was so powerfully salient that in his mind, it must be shared by others unless they are just down-right mean.

Branching off this concept leads us to precausal thinking, or transductive reasoning, where a child in their early years has an incomplete understanding of cause and effect that results in a relationship being drawn between two separate events that are unrelated. "The dog barked and made my balloon pop." Or believing that something bad happened to their father because they were thinking bad thoughts of him. One can start to imagine how this surfaces in situations of early life traumatic experiences, including loss.

Just for teens

So that I do not mislead you into thinking the fun stuff only takes place during the first few years, here are a few adolescent concepts that may help answer some questions. Elkind (1967) expanded on what we learned from Piaget around egocentrism. There is a heightened intensity in adolescence around how the teens think of themselves and how they think about what others may be thinking of them. If they think others do not like them, they view themselves as being despised. If they are good at something, they me feel unique and special. Elkind termed imaginary audience as when the teen now believes that everything they do is on display to others. In their minds, their new pimple or stain on their shirt is noticed and talked about by their peers.

Elkind's personal fable is the teen having a distorted view of their own importance or feeling as if their experience is unique and that no one could possibly understand. No one knows what it is like to be me. Even a simple exchange between a parent and teen with the best of intentions can go array. Think of the conversation where the parent tries to comfort the teen going through a breakup and trying to relate and normalize it by talking about their experience and attempting to instill hope for future relationships. The teen is adamant that the parent can't understand because their breakup is different. Their situation is different- any adults relate to this if you think back to being that teen? But we forget what it was like at that time and grow up and give the same well-intended conversations. And I do not think it means that we stop showing support in this way, yet we do it with a slightly different lens of what their experience may be.

Next, we have this concept of the illusion of invulnerability or the invincibility fable. Or as I call it the 'it's not going to happen to me' phenomenon. This, coupled with the fact that our brain's frontal lobes are not fully developed until our early to mid-twenties can help explain some of the decision making in that timeframe. You will learn about the frontal lobe in a later section. When we are teenagers, we all make some questionable decisions and I think we forget that when we become adults. And we forget about the challenges that teens are really faced with as they are sandwiched in between the expectations of remaining a respectful, obedient, and dutiful child and sheltered under the umbrella of a parent's protection yet, looking for them to behave like adults with problem solving and autonomous thinking. The cognitive demands are intense as they rely more on their amygdala (you will see this emotional part in the brain section) because their part that manages impulse control, decision making, planning, and judgment are not fully intact until early adulthood.

Then you add on societal and family demands while setting them up for sleep deprivation as we ignore science that shows their circadian rhythm requires additional sleep in the early to mid-morning for optimal functioning (maybe until 10am). Some adults and teachers assume that their teens are sleepy during the day because of staying up all night on their phones chatting or surfing the internet. While that can be true at times for some, for others there is a biological reason for it. I could put together a giant section on the impact of sleep deprivation and go into all the areas in depth but will save you from that to not veer off topic too far. I do realize that there would be other factors to consider in adjusting school start times in how it impacts the caregiver's work schedule for one. However, if we did adjust when they begin school it would reduce health risks and improve learning. Not to mention how it would positively impact their mood, which disperses into the household. Whether you have 8 people living in a house or two, you know how one person's mood impacts another and the ripple effects that ensue.

I wish I could sell you that proverbial bubble that we wish we could put our children in. I would really give it away free if I had the design and product and then I would be contradicting some of what I say later around our experiences and pain building so many other attributes and traits that are so positive and useful to us later. Something that can be discouraging to parents is that our teens become most vulnerable to peer influence between the ages of 12 and 14. Fear of rejection from the group can increase conformity and striving to fit in. We can teach our kids that it is more important to find where they belong, where people accept them for who they are. We also need to listen and validate how hard that may be so we can show we get it, which can foster additional communication in the relationship. Remember, although our teens are naturally coming into their independence, they still need (and want) their parental figures. We just have to keep in mind that it is through an experience of connection rather than us attempting to control them. I am sure we can all think of our experiences where we learned this the hard way.

Some of you may be parents experiencing traumatic wounds from having a teen who may struggle with substance use, and the aftermath of any trauma related precipitants or consequences of their use. Tremendous loss and pain from losing the relationship you once had with your child due to mental health or substance abuse challenges, incarceration, or having passed away from an overdose, can hit you in places where and when you least expect it or where you just are not ready for it. This is when you find yourself staring at the Toaster Strudels in the freezer section of the supermarket with tears coming down because that was your child's favorite breakfast food and now you have no reason to put it in your cart.

So many of you have questioned a thousand times what went wrong, where you could have done something different. This piece of information around being vulnerable to peers (and all the other environmental influences) also reminds us that there is no perfect world and that we can be great parents, and still not be the only ones that our children hear, see, and encounter. With that, we need to give ourselves some grace as no one is perfect. We are great at having compassion for others but not so good when turning that inward.

Early development of emotional experience and regulation

Understanding one's early emotional and attachment development may also be useful as you explore certain areas of impact of trauma. We know that emotion plays a significant role in higher order cognitive processing (the more complex and sophisticated thinking and reasoning) and without it we lack resourcefulness. Emotions serve us in playing a significant role in communication and are important for our cognitive functioning. A lot of people once believed that emotions cloud one's ability for logical decision making yet some research notes compelling evidence that the absence of emotion will impair cognition rather than enhance it, and it has an additional level of regulation of behavior (Damasio, 1994; Damasio & Carvalho, 2013). Emotions play a role in higher-order cognitive functioning like mentioned previously in the prefrontal cortex. They help with memory, decision making, and planful behavior. Damasio and Carvalho (2013) have noted that "some of the most pressing health issues we face today, such as depression, drug addiction and intractable pain, are centered on pathologies of feeling. Elucidating the physiology of feeling states therefore has exceptional biomedical relevance (p.143)."

Emotions serve us in the form of protection and survival; they are a signal to us in many ways which is why I try to steer away from labeling certain emotions as being the "negative" ones. Think about the fear elicited in a dangerous situation that helps us engage our instinctual response (of fight, flight, freeze, or feigned death that will be touched on later), or even at the disgust of certain materials or toxic bacteria that keep us from it and away from harm. We also see this in the emotional affect (facial expression) that is elicited in babies that encourage a nurturing and caring response from their caregiver.

There is value in emotions for our overall mental health and so much so, that Salovey and Mayer (1990) coined the term emotional intelligence, to mean one's ability to monitor their own and others' feelings and emotions, to be able to discriminate among them and to use this information to guide their own thinking and actions. Emotions are seen as distinct from mood as they are generally more intense and shorter as they are in response to an event (internal or external) and are influenced by a cognitive meaning attached to it by the individual. Those with greater emotional intelligence have been correlated with greater self-regulation, greater life satisfaction, and increased psychological and social well-being (Extremera & Rey, 2016).

There are several theories of emotion, each having their own research and debates over others, that vary from believing we infer emotions from physiology- I'm sad because I am crying, emotions and arousal occur simultaneously- our trembling happens at the same time we feel afraid, and emotion is a combination of physical arousal with a simultaneous cognitive appraisal (the way we label it in our thoughts). Some argue that physiological arousal is the same for a wide variety of emotions (i.e., increased heart rate can be experienced if you are anxious, angry, scared, excited, or surprised) so that alone cannot be responsible for the emotional response. Infants have emotional contagion in the first few weeks of life and is thought of as their first ability to detect emotion in others. A classic example is the cry from one baby in a childcare facility that sets off a firestorm of multiple crying babies. Any childcare staff readers or caregivers of multiple infants at one time I am sure are relating to this. By about three months of age, they start to imitate facial expressions of caregivers.

Many ascribe to the idea that basic emotions include joy/happiness, sadness, anger, disgust, and fear, while others may add in surprise or interest to the list. It is not until around 18-24 months that they start to show outward signs of jealousy, empathy, and embarrassment, and then around 30-36 months the shame, guilt, and pride can be seen. This reflects their ability around that time to use social standards and rules to evaluate their own behaviors. This comes with two major cognitive and emotional advances of representational thought and emotional response to wrongdoing. I would like to briefly note the difference between the emotions of shame and guilt in sample thoughts of "I am a bad person" versus "I did a bad thing" respectively. In treatment we see numerous patients struggle with either, or both, often driven by underlying messages picked up in our younger years of the Just-World fallacy. We will revisit this in a section later when discussing the impact of trauma on our cognitions.

Initially, it is caregivers that scaffold the development of emotion regulation. Their interactions become synchronous and reciprocal. Dr. Edward Tronick is well-known for his Still-Face Experiment in the 1970s that helps us understand the importance of these early interactions in infants attempting to achieve connection in their relational world. Anyone reading this can search for relevant videos online and get a glimpse at the reaction of the baby when the mother is not responding and keeps her face still. The baby's distress heightens, and she relies on her own self-directed coping of rubbing her hair, looking away, rocking, and sucking. Older infants (around ten months) begin to engage in social referencing, where they base their emotional reactions on caregivers' behaviors. The child uses the adult's emotions and affective display to discern meaning from, and in, events, and to intuit information about the self. They begin to rely on them for support and cues on how to proceed. They are also becoming aware of themselves as a social agent and their emotion regulation improves with age.

The development of self is not clearly demarcated and is a gradual process. Self-recognition, or objective self-awareness begins around 18 months of age. In cultures with more relational interactions and less independence emphasized, as seen in more collectivistic communities, development is a little later as it is less important to focus on the self in separate. Maltreated children show more negative or neutral affect when looking at themselves in a mirror, not surprising to learn.

The self-concept which includes gender identity, race, ethnicity, and skin color are typically recognized by age three. Children of color tend to recognize some of these faster as race is a primary dimension referred to when describing people, innate or learned. And coupled with a variety of environmental and social exchanges can influence race-based traumatic stress (coined by Dr. Robert Carter in 2007) stemming from experiences with racial bias and discrimination resulting in negative mental and physical/medical health outcomes. The self-concept gets even more impacted when considering the intersection of those who belong to multiple oppressed or marginalized groups including race, gender, ethnicity, and sexuality that can in and of itself be felt as traumatic based on a variety of experiences.

Attachment formation and its implications

You may notice that around eight months of age (remember I did say it was a busy time) an infant starts to display anxiety to strangers or unfamiliar faces. They have a schema for familiar faces and when these unfamiliar faces do not assimilate into that schema, they get frightened. This is a new ability at this age to evaluate people. There is a bond of attachment that is developed between an infant and their caregiver that is built internally to help protect that child.

Children were once thought of as becoming attached to those individuals who solely provided nourishment to them, yet this was debunked accidentally in Harlow's experiments with infant monkeys (Harlow et al., 1971). He showed that they became attached to the warmth and nurturance that the cloth-covered wire monkeys provided over the monkeys built out of wire with no cloth covering that had a bottle attached. Their intense attachment to the cloth-coverings contradicted the idea that attachment derives from an association with nourishment. One could say this was an encouraging discovery for those caregivers who did not engage in breastfeeding, that they could absolutely establish a strong bond in the absence of that, as it is the nurturance and warmth that matters in the initial attachment bond.

What does attachment have to do with it? Depending on who you ask, some would say everything. Erik Erikson and John Bowlby are just two people who studied child development, and both emphasize the importance of the caregiving relationship on the child's view, or working model, of themselves and others. It has later implications for one's self-concept and outlook on life. Children need to establish a sense of basic trust, that their world is reliable and predictable. The type of early parenting or caregiving received can influence whether a child approaches life (from childhood into adulthood) with an attitude of trust, as seen in securely attached children, or one of fear.

Bowlby believed that connections emerge in stages but are full-fledged around 7-8 months. Mary Ainsworth is known for her studies in the late 1970s that have been replicated over the years to help inform us of the nature of a secure vs an insecure attachment and what the implications of that may be. These are terms often explored in trauma related research and treatment. Fortunately, we do know that most children are securely attached and that can be seen across cultures. Yet, those who fall into the insecurely attached group, have reverberations across their lifespan and oftentimes are even unaware of their own attachment styles.

We know there is a reciprocal relationship with the influence that a child's temperament has on a parent's response and the consequences of caregiving styles. So, what does a secure attachment look like? If you can picture a mom leaving a room that her child is in, we would see that the child is distressed by the separation and starts crying or whining as they watch her walk away. That would be expected; the key is to notice the interaction when the mom returns and, in this case, they are seeking closeness with her and wanting to be held and comforted. They are then able to wipe away their tears and return to their play. Securely attached children believe that their caregivers will be there for them when they need them.

For insecurely attached children, their response looks much different when mom returns. They may become sullen or closed off and unwelcoming or unresponsive to mom's attempts at comfort. They may become physically aggressive at mom's attempt to soothe, i.e., the mom tries to hand them a toy they like to make them feel better and they push their mom's arm away.

Avoidant (aka dismissive) attachment can follow parenting that is emotionally distant where they don't tolerate expression of emotions. These caregivers may also have been insensitive or have engaged in ridiculing or ignoring. As they grow older, these children grow up to be fearful or avoidant of and in relationships. They are likely to appear self-confident and struggle to tolerate their own emotional or physical intimacy. They place more value on independence and aren't very interested in forming deep/close relationships. It may include distraction seeking, suppression of feelings, and even acting defensively with others.

Individuals with ambivalent (aka preoccupied/anxious) attachment have often experienced caregiving that is inconsistent, unpredictable, or self-centered. As children, they may cry for the adult even before separation happens. When the adult returns, they may show anger. They may have a heightened or exaggerated response to get the attention of the adult at home. As adults we see them clinging to their relationships and when perceiving threats become reactive or demanding. They may need constant reassurance from their intimate partners as they fear rejection and abandonment. They often grown up into adults who question their worth and fear they aren't good enough.

Disorganized (aka fearful avoidant) attachment typically results when the child's caregivers become a source of fear likely because of abuse. This is often the most challenging in treatment as we see they want closeness yet they're afraid of it. In adulthood, these individuals believe that rejection is inevitable, that their partner can't possibly love them as they are. They may choose a partner that rightfully brings on fear which leads them to believe they are right that others can't be trusted. And a person with this attachment style may very well get the rejection they are expecting from others because they start to act in ways that can elicit their partner pulling away; maybe there is an intensity or unpredictability about their behavior.

Consistency in responding to a child is what has been essential to the secure attachment, in responding to the child's needs. Remember this connects to that object constancy noted earlier; if developed, the child will grow up to trust the stability in a relationship even when things aren't always good or in physical distance. If not, they can be consumed by worry that they will be rejected.

As my husband words it- you don't spoil kids (with consistent attention), you spoil food. The child needs to rely on the caregiver as a secure base that allows them to feel the confidence to explore their world around them. When a child's attachment figure (caregiver, parent) is the source of the threat, the child becomes conflicted internally around what is safer- to push that attachment figure and others away, or to attach. Both the idea or act of separation and the connection do not feel safe to that child.

Caregivers both directly and indirectly influence the development of their children through their behavior, actions, and the things that are verbalized to them. Children also influence their caregivers by their behaviors, interests, and attitudes. There are two dimensions that we typically speak of in parental behavior that include 1. control and 2. warmth and/or responsiveness. The spectrum of control can range from being domineering or acting like a puppeteer, setting reasonable standards and expectations and monitoring, to having little to no standards or expectations at all. For warmth and responsiveness someone can be openly warm and affectionate, responding to their emotional needs, to the other direction of being relatively uninvolved emotionally and feeling bothered by their display of emotion and affect.

These dimensions are absolutely impacted by cultural factors that can include how emotional display is viewed, level of acculturation and socioeconomic status, and can vary not only from one household to the next, but we can also see that in homes with two caregivers there can be a difference between them. The way these dimensions intersect influence the responses seen in the children.

Some caregivers may want the best for their child so badly that they start to believe they need to give in to whatever the child wants to keep them happy. I have seen very well-intended caregivers with this approach that end up kicking themselves later wondering why their child doesn't listen, is impulsive or immature, and gets in trouble a lot. Think about it, if we don't set some structure, guidance, and parameters that help the child learn how to manage their behaviors and how they get their needs met, it isn't a surprise that they don't know how to do it later for themselves. When we ignore their emotional needs and lack nurturance it can help explain several developments like opposition and aggression.

Parenting styles are often part of the exploration when clients are in therapy working on family of origin issues and how their upbringing contributes to current struggles. Our aim is not to point a finger or blame caregivers and looking at all of this can help us make some sense out of things. Knowing these early life contributions may help one begin to understand why trauma that happens in early childhood (regardless of if it is a caregiver, friend, professional, or stranger) can leave a deeper wound that often needs a distinctive style of treatment than one that happens in later adulthood.

Section 2

What is Trauma

So now that we have a foundation of a few developmental concepts and processes, how do we understand what trauma even is? Before defining that let me first say that the word *trauma* is used for ease of writing a little more succinctly yet, a lot of what is included in this book can apply to what may be more preferably termed *adverse experiences*. We do not need you to meet the following definition of posttraumatic stress disorder (PTSD), complex posttraumatic stress disorder (CPTSD), dissociative identity disorder (DID), or any of the examples given to represent trauma to be able to benefit from the material.

Trauma is obviously not a new concept, yet we are seeing an increase in statistics of what people are experiencing and for children, it is bullying, maltreatment by a caregiver, domestic violence, and witnessing violent acts. This obviously does not have one clear cause and can involve influences from the microsystemic level of immediate environment with a child being raised by a parent who abuses substances or a caregiver with unmet mental health needs, to socioeconomic factors of poverty and unsafe living conditions, and cultural experiences of growing up with unhealthy dynamics and modeling of power and control, and so on.

We are seeing a shift in recognizing and acknowledging what can be viewed as trauma (we still have some people who think that only a war veteran gets PTSD) and our field is making progress in helping people feel more comfortable talking about it and seeking help. I once heard a colleague describe trauma as too much sensation happening too fast with too little warning. What I hope to continue is not just the progress in what our field recognizes, but what an individual is able to recognize for themselves. Patients, friends, family members, colleagues, you name it- I have heard so many make comments around their experience not being as bad as some others and so they should not be affected by it, thus they don't seek support or therapy.

There are different versions of what is considered traumatic. Trauma can be subjective as no two people perceive and respond to a situation in the exact same way. Some examples that are typically thought of as having the potential to be traumatic are serious illness or a complication with a medical procedure or a botched surgery; significant physical pain, or an injury (maybe from a car accident or a fall); domestic abuse/violence; sexual assault; terrorism, being involved in war, life as a refugee; natural disaster; and witnessing violence or a death.

Loss and subsequent grief can be viewed as traumatic and can depend on a few things like the way the person died (cause) and their perception of death and its meaning. And loss also does not equate with death as maybe you have an experience with a loved one being incarcerated; think of the last embrace as you feel the person being pulled away or not even getting to have any notice as you learn of it over the phone. Then you are faced with all the consequences that follow in managing life without them and potentially managing other lives that may have depended on them. Top that off with the anxiety and fear of their safety and knowledge of how dignity often goes out the window when behind bars. Or loss of the relationship as you imagined it when you learn of infidelity or of a new medical condition in a partner that changes the dreams you had for yourself and as a couple. This is by no means an exhaustive list and you may have a history with trauma and adverse experiences that are not here in print.

There are individuals who experience what is known as a single incident event, meaning they have experienced one traumatic event. There are many others who are more familiar with undergoing what is termed complex trauma that involve more chronic or cumulative encounters with traumatic events (multiple events). Although for many they have an onset in early life, there are individuals with no significant childhood history finding themselves as survivors of complex trauma in adulthood. Another term you might see is developmental trauma which is thought of as chronic experiences mentioned here that have an onset in early childhood and typically occur over extended periods of time and have an interpersonal element as they often occur within the context of closer relationships. After learning just a few pieces of early childhood development one can see how the abuse, neglect, or other maltreatment that takes place in those early years where there are vulnerable stages of life can have long-term implications and leave an individual to be more susceptible and at risk for subsequent stressors and adverse experiences later in life.

Complex/developmental traumas often involve betrayal or profound violation of human connection, rights, and trust. Examples can include (again not a full list) chronic neglect or abandonment, ongoing physical/sexual/emotional/verbal abuse, human trafficking, bullying, dysfunctional home environments, and chronic experiences with racism/discrimination. Someone who is in the throes of an addiction can be experiencing trauma both directly and indirectly related to their use. Parentification can also be seen through a lens of complex trauma, where a child takes on an adult role which can be for a variety of reasons and can be seen frequently in those households where children grow up with parents who are in active substance use.

Another example could be moving from one foster family to another being equally traumatic as the initial abuse the child experienced that resulted in the placement in the first place. Here, a child often learns the world is an extremely dangerous place and they must think "every person for themselves" bringing on a need to become the toughest kid around for self-preservation. Not a far stretch to bring in some behavioral disorders. I once was employed as a child abuse investigator for the Department of Children and Families in Florida and can remember the confusion early in the role of feeling like I had a purpose in protecting children as I had to remove some from their home environments, yet the pain that I simultaneously was a part of as the children are ripped from their world that to them still felt safe and familiar. I think about the family trauma on all generations who are faced with struggles around immigration and deportation as they are just trying to have the safety that every human seeks. Even experiences with your own mental health and substance use diagnoses and the consequences of them, or a loved one's, can be viewed through a lens of trauma.

A colloquial distinction of "big T" and "little T" trauma has floated around in our field and you may have heard it in the public, with the "big T" events being something like a violent crime, shooting, or death of a parent. Whereas, "little T" may be used for some experiences noted that get looked at as complex trauma. However, the field is not in total agreement about the use of these terms as it has been both received and delivered in ways that come across as invalidating or minimizing and has the potential to imply that someone else's experience is more significant.

And being referred to as little may also suggest that it doesn't have much of an impact when we know that they can have significant and long-standing impacts. As Brickel (2019) stated in her blog, "you can't necessarily see the bruises, but these things are just as damaging." She also proposes "obvious" vs "hidden" trauma as the language if we must make the distinction. I am often talking about our mind's attempts at efficiency by boxing things into categories when I am teaching about diversity and multicultural issues. But it isn't any different here in trauma and in our mental health field overall, that we need to be careful because the desire for efficiency ends up leading to inaccuracies and gross negligence when it comes to understanding people at the most fundamental human level.

About 20% to a third of people who experience trauma go on to develop PTSD. This also means that a good percentage of people do not. About a third may develop acute stress disorder which involves symptoms of PTSD that only last up to a month at maximum. And about a third or more of the people who live through trauma will not go on to develop trauma related symptoms. I am hesitant to use the term resilient for this latter group of people because even the individuals who develop PTSD and other trauma related diagnoses can be viewed as being quite resilient in finding ways to adapt and survive.

In knowing the aforementioned statistics, I always encourage clinicians and students to be mindful of being symptom driven rather than event driven in terms of making an actual diagnosis. Something can be traumatic and not result in a mental health diagnosis, so it is important to remember this to not discount or minimize someone's experience that they may be sharing just because they aren't symptomatic from it, yet also not to assign pathology where there isn't any. This can be true for loved ones in how easy it is to think "oh my, there is no way they can be ok after living through that." Or the counter to that of being dismissive and surprised that someone is struggling to move forward in their life after having gone through something very painful.

No two people are alike in the way they interpret an event. Yet, people will always have judgment and their opinions, and we are not strangers to the comment we often hear about that goes a little something like "C'mon put your big pants on and deal with it, everyone goes through things; that was ten years ago so let it go already!" Sound familiar? Has that helped you yet? Has that helped anyone you may have told that to yet? My guess is no. Nonetheless, experiences become traumatic when they overwhelm our ability to cope. While the symptoms of situational stress that many of us may be familiar with – sadness, hopelessness, fear, anxiety, diminished interest in social activities or trouble sleeping – may mimic the symptoms of a response to unresolved trauma, they are far less likely to be associated with problems functioning at work, at school, or other everyday situations.

Trauma symptoms/diagnoses

PTSD is a mental health diagnosis that could develop after trauma yet is not the definition of trauma. As for defining the diagnosis of post-traumatic stress disorder, the 5th edition of the Diagnostic and Statistical Manual (DSM-5) defines it as having exposure to actual or threatened death, serious injury, or sexual violence either directly or indirectly with specific symptoms directly related to the event. Remember, that is the criteria for a diagnosis of PTSD and not the definition of trauma itself.

While a PTSD diagnosis involves many of the same symptoms as situational stress, there are four categories of symptoms that are particular to a PTSD diagnosis: Intrusive memory and recall; avoidance; negative alterations in cognition and mood; and arousal and reactivity. To receive a diagnosis of PTSD, these criteria must be present for at least a month, and they must cause significant distress or impairment in social, occupational, or other key areas of functioning. If the duration is less than a month, a person may instead have an acute stress disorder, which has similar symptoms but a shortened experience. Here, simple stress-busting techniques like exercise, meditation, healthy eating, or counseling may help significantly.

Please remember though that you may have symptoms that follow here yet not meet the criteria in full for this diagnosis and another trauma and stressor related disorder may be the more appropriate category. One can experience something traumatic and have more subtle impacts that don't necessarily fit these next paragraphs very neatly and one may still need some support even if not diagnosable. An example of this could be going through collective trauma that I will define and further explain separately later. Trauma symptoms do not show up the same in everyone, so I do give a little caution as you read through the symptoms that you do not try to box your loved one (or yourself) into what is presented here.

The first criterion I am reviewing requires the presence of at least one intrusion symptom which really involves re-experiencing the event in several ways and can include nightmares, intrusive recall, flashbacks, and becoming highly distressed when thinking of it. Intrusive symptoms are behind what is often labeled a "trauma response," which has been a term used to describe behaviors and reactions in situations that may seem out of proportion to the observer or not warranted for what has just transpired. You will learn the impact of trauma on the brain later and how this can happen where one's rational decision making goes out the proverbial window.

One of the hallmarks of a trauma response is intrusive recall, where a thought or an image related to the trauma experience will suddenly intrude, even in the most unexpected moments. This can be debilitating. The thoughts can be about themselves or the person that was involved in the trauma, perhaps where it took place, or other details. For example, if a child was mocked or screamed at during dinner, the intrusive image may be what his plate looked like just before the rage escalated, or his father's disgruntled face. Intrusive recall also happens in the form of nightmares. It is not always a nightmare that involves that specific trauma, but it may have similar content or themes. Perhaps the trauma was sexual abuse, but the nightmares are not necessarily about sexual abuse, they are about being held down and not being able to get up, or not being able to move in a situation – the feeling of powerlessness. It could involve a general theme of trying to run away from someone.

The other intrusive symptom we see frequently is dissociation, where a person is physically present but seems to have checked out mentally, like they are not even in the room. Often, they are visualizing and feeling as if they are in that experience all over again. The part of their brain that keeps track of "the here and now" is confused about whether what they are feeling is a memory or something happening in the present. In that situation we use grounding techniques, reorienting the person to the room and their present environment to get them out of the dissociation. I will mention some grounding exercises in a later section. Trauma rewires the brain and people cannot just "snap out of it." They may need therapy and tools to help them safely manage their emotions and cope in a healthy way.

The next criterion requires an avoidance of or efforts to avoid distressing thoughts, feelings, or memories associated with the event and/or external reminders of the event that could be people, places, activities, objects, etc. Avoidance is trying to run from it, ignore it, or trying not to have it and time can be something that impacts whether someone is presenting with PTSD symptoms. The intensity of emotional pain often reduces with time. However, this can be tricky if the time is filled up with avoidance. This is when one tries so hard to resist thinking about the trauma, resisting the emotional pain, or avoiding certain places or reminders and this contrarily results in longer term suffering.

Running away from your problems is a race that you will never win. It is as if one's brain is thinking "If there is not a threat then why is my person trying so hard not to think or feel something?" and so it thinks "I guess I should hang on to this to help warn me." How many things have you tried to bury away in your mind; it does not change the reality of its existence. We try so hard to re-write the narrative of past events, but the hard truth is that we can't. And a lot of us get stuck in this, with trauma and life events in general. Looking at this closely, those events never really become your past because you are continuing to live in it/fight in it as your present. And with the right treatment and support it does not have to stay this way.

People especially try to avoid unpleasant emotions via distraction techniques and often substance use. Many are afraid of what will happen once they feel them as mentioned earlier. I often try to help patients see how emotions that are felt and processed can indeed be lessened through the analogy of a shaken up carbonated beverage. If we open the lid it starts to explode, and we so quickly try to tighten it back up to hold it in. But if we keep the lid off, it may pour over and then what? - it eventually settles. And we help them understand that emotions serve a purpose- that they are messengers of information that guide our decisions and actions (help keep us safe), tell who we are (likes and dislikes), and communicate with others.

The criterion of Mood and Cognitive changes involve emotions of shame, guilt, horror, fear, anger, and an inability to experience positive emotions. It also includes having distorted cognitions and self-blame. Patients often have thoughts of the trauma being their fault "If I had only _____ (fill in the blank), then this would not have happened." Or thoughts about what this must mean about them as a person. One's perception of the event can then become more powerful than the event itself in terms of what it may mean about them as a person, or what it means about others, or even what it says about the world in general. This can have individuals believing that they are damaged, they'll never be able to feel safe, will never have fulfilling relationships, are going to suffer for the rest of their lives, and that the world is a dangerous place. Now one may argue at this moment that there is indeed danger out there in the world, yet the belief as written implies an all-or-nothing message that there is nothing else but danger. We will focus more specifically on this thought process in a later section.

The last of the criteria requires two or more symptoms related to arousal and reactivity. You may have heard of the term hyperarousal and hypoarousal. Hyper is a prefix that means exaggerated, beyond, over, or in excess whereas hypo means low, below, or under what is normal. A few examples of hyperarousal are being overly vigilant, aware of surroundings, easily startled, problems concentrating, and heightened attention to body states/somatic (soma=body) symptoms. Some people find difficulty in falling asleep while others it may show up as problems staying asleep. Irritability/anger outbursts are also included here. Whereas hypoarousal may be shutting down or going numb physically and emotionally.

You may have heard the terms way back in a high school science class even of fight, flight, and freeze. Well, we have fight, flight, and freeze as hyperarousal symptoms. Some may add in a cry for help as hyperarousal that could look like heightened eye contact, seeking proximity, and getting on the phone and calling a loved one to connect. Some of you reading this may think I made a typo by putting freeze as a state of hyperarousal, so here it is explained. Ogden (2006) refers to it as alert immobility when there is activity arrest and the body is constricted and tense, like a paralyzed fear. This freeze can be high arousal just coupled with immobility. The freeze that some of you may be thinking of for hypoarousal is also referred to as feigned death that can be observed as flat affect, decreased sensation, slowed movement, collapsed posture, limp muscles, and being unresponsive. It is an immobility physically without the anxiety and high internal arousal previously mentioned.

Complex trauma does not have its own separate label for diagnosis yet in the DSM-5, so some of you reading this may come across a diagnosis written something like "PTSD, complex/developmental" in a written report which helps the next clinician reading it gauge the direction of treatment. However, it has found a place in the International Classification of Diseases (ICD-11) as CPTSD. PTSD and CPTSD fall under the same category in the ICD-11 of *Disorders specifically related to stress*. It is most commonly a result of prolonged or repetitive events of an extremely horrific or threatening nature.

CPTSD includes the ICD-11's three core elements of their definition of PTSD that is similar to the DSM-5, plus three additional pieces related to disturbances in self-organization. The first of these three elements are having problems with affect regulation- think of expressing emotion. This may look like heightened emotional reactivity to minor stressors, reckless or self-destructive behavior, and those violent outbursts like the "Hulk Rage" event I mentioned in the intro. It could also include having an experience where one feels detached, out of body, or has a loss of memory, which we refer to as dissociative symptoms. Emotional numbing falls in this umbrella as well. This individual has difficulty experiencing pleasure or positive emotions.

Second, is having diminished beliefs about oneself in feeling defeated or worthless, accompanied by feelings of shame/guilt/ failure related to the traumatic event. This may seem confusing to the outsider who is clearly able to see that it isn't that person's fault. But for the survivor, they may feel guilty for not escaping sooner or for not preventing the abuse. And the third is difficulty sustaining relationships and feeling close to others. It could range from avoidance of intimacy to intensely seeking closeness. We will explore these further in later sections.

Cloitre (2020) notes that studies have found that someone can get a diagnosis of CPTSD with a single incident trauma in their history, just as someone with chronic trauma like child abuse can develop PTSD. The author shared that these observations shed some light on the influence of dispositional factors like genetic make-up, and environmental factors that could be the presence or lack of social support.

Dissociative Identity Disorder (DID) is another diagnosis that is often associated with a history of trauma. This diagnosis involves a disruption of identity characterized by two or more distinct personalities (DSM-5, 2013). It impacts one's sense of self, affect, behavior, consciousness, perception, cognition, and memory. There may be memory gaps for personal data, everyday events, and even of the trauma itself that are not typical of forgetfulness. NAMI (2022) points out that dissociative disorders typically develop to help the individual deal with their trauma and are most common in those who experience prolonged childhood abuse. The average age when symptoms begin to show is 16 yet they can begin in early to mid-childhood and are possible yet not as common to begin after the age of 20. I have read two fascinating books of real accounts of DID both involving a history of trauma (Oxnam, 2005 & Baer, 2007). You can check these out in the References section for additional reading. Other excellent resources are from Carolyn Spring (2016 & 2019).

There may also be dissociation without having DID as it is more of a state of being disconnected. We may see it show up as them speaking about their past experiences yet without any emotion tied to it. Brickel (2020) understands that dissociation is sometimes the best way the person can survive something traumatic and terrifying yet, reminds us that it interferes with forming secure connections, or being fully present in these relationships. These individuals may not even be aware of their experience with dissociation.

Children may look different

It is astounding to know that 26% of children in the US will witness or experience a traumatic event before they turn 4 (Briggs-Gowan, et. al., 2010). Looking at that developmentally, children are building their roadmap for life at an incredibly early age, and their brain processes information very differently than adults. Trauma that happens in childhood runs the risk of leaving more of a mark in their expectations of self, other people, and the world. And just like children are little scientists, constantly attempting to make sense of their world, they may make meaning out of something they experience that isn't true and it can have a lasting impact. Therefore, trauma that happens as a child vs an adult may have a difference in how the person thinks, feels, and behaves.

Children may not have the language to articulate their experience to explain their shifts in responses, thoughts, and emotions to themselves, let alone a school professional for example when being questioned about their performance in the classroom or to their parent at home when they are displaying moodiness. Additionally, their attempts at meeting a need for connection and continuously seeking the nurturance and safety they were denied, often gets labeled attention seeking.

Yet is it attention seeking? Frankly I still think that could be used if it weren't so associated with a negative perception as it makes sense to me that kids who were neglected for example would want to try to get attention anywhere they could find it. What child doesn't need attention? However, because of the connotation of that label, it may be more aptly named 'attachment seeking.' Children with a history of trauma may be more vulnerable to feelings of alienation and loneliness. They may over-react to what others see as minor upsets, create distractions when adults are trying to do other things, or maybe they are always trying to be helpful. We may also see them talk a lot which can involve asking many questions and even telling tall tales.

Forbes (2017) provides a list of 10 behaviors that are common when children don't know how to express their needs verbally. She provides some interpretation behind them in helping readers understand the message being conveyed by them. She poses cursing as a way for the child to "jar the parent's nervous system into listening." They may also engage in this behavior out of fear of not being good enough for that parent's attention. Slamming doors is looked at through the lens of needing to have a voice and being heard. Hitting another sibling is often thought of as an issue between the two kids, yet it is often more about the relationship the child holds with the parent/s. Even though he/she may get scolded by the parent, "to a child with a trauma history, any form of attention, whether positive or negative, is love."

A child may shut down by way of losing eye contact, giving the silent treatment, or walking away. Forbes continues to point out our misinterpretation with this being seen as defiance when it is really them feeling overwhelmed. It may be their self-preservation in the moment. Challenging authority may not be a surprise when you think about how a child's trauma may come from someone who was supposed to care for them or protect them. So, the child who is argumentative is coming from a place of mistrust. Arguing is also a way of staying connected to a parent and not wanting the exchange to end.

The child who shouts words like 'I hate you' is maybe struggling with their own self-hatred and seeing it as easier to hurt someone else than feel internal pain. Pushing boundaries is more of a test or challenge that the child is hoping that parent will meet, in not giving up on them. When a child seems to be struggling during a time of transition in their life or home, their fear is that something bad is going to happen just like it did in their past. Even transitions that are positive and will bring goodness can be scary. And lastly, Forbes presents laziness as a "gross misinterpretation of the child." This is more of a form of learned helplessness where they learned that their efforts didn't result in change. A child that experienced neglect, and no matter what they tried they couldn't get their parent to respond in the way they needed, no longer sees any worth or value in trying anymore.

Health impact

Felitti et. al. (1998) performed a study on thousands of adults asking about adverse experiences they had as a child and then compared it to measures of adult risk behavior, disease, and health status. This Adverse Childhood Experiences (ACE) study has been widely utilized and referenced and I encourage anyone reading to visit the Center for Disease Control and Prevention website to learn more. You will find a short video talking about how we can prevent ACEs as well as other facts, data, strategies, and resources.

Unresolved trauma can have a mighty impact on a person's health. And I say unresolved trauma because it is possible to heal and move beyond trauma. During stress, the body responds by stimulating the adrenal glands to produce cortisol, adrenaline, and noradrenaline to help us prepare for action in times of danger. These hormones can even show up in times of worry. They play a vital role in keeping you safe, but they are not meant to circulate in the bloodstream for prolonged periods of time. Extreme, prolonged stress may diminish your body's ability to perform at its full capacity, which can lead to physical or mental health symptoms including burnout. Burnout can leave you disinterested in work, reckless, tense, and forgetful, with difficulty concentrating.

Someone who has experienced trauma may have stronger and more frequent surges of adrenaline from their heightened responses and perception of danger, which causes wear and tear on the body. Unresolved trauma puts people at increased risk for mental health diagnoses, which run the gamut of anxiety, depression, and PTSD. There are physical manifestations as well, such as cardiovascular problems like high blood pressure, stroke, or heart attacks. There has been research to connect unresolved trauma to fibromyalgia and general inflammation in the body, which can lead to autoimmune disorders and organ fibrosis. Obesity and cancer are also associated with unresolved trauma. Unresolved trauma puts people at higher risk of substance use disorder, as substance use is often initiated or increased after trauma.

Protective factors

It was noted earlier that not everyone who experiences trauma go on to develop PTSD. We are often talking about risk factors for example, how adverse childhood experiences coupled with a lack of social support and few resources may contribute to a physical or mental health condition. Some fans discuss how the Hulk wasn't simply born out of his gamma ray exposure. He experienced his own trauma as a child, ranging from abuse if you are referencing the television series or witnessing his father kill his mother if we are talking about present day films. We have our biology, neurochemicals, and genetics accounting for something but not everything, our environmental experiences and our psychological mindset have interaction effects.

Thankfully, several studies, literature, and blogs devoted to the topic of trauma speak about this thing we call protective factors. They are characteristics and other influences that lower the chances of negative outcomes. Finding a way to help others in their healing process has given many a sense of value and purpose. Continuous contact with, and support from, important people in one's life can make a difference. This is also something that during the pandemic with social distancing may have required more creativity and effort to maintain. The support also includes the survivor being able and comfortable disclosing the trauma to a loved one. The identification of oneself as a survivor as opposed to a victim may seem like a trivial language shift, yet we know language is important in how we see ourselves and others. Each of those labels allows for their own implied messages to come right along with them.

Another essential piece that is protective in nature is holding the belief that you can manage your feelings and cope.

SECTION 3

$\mathcal{U}$nderstanding $\mathcal{T}$he $\mathcal{B}$rain

First just some basics

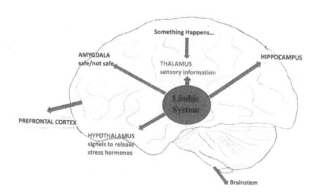

There is no question that experiencing trauma impacts our brain, it is just that a lot of people (especially if not in any treatment) are not informed of what really happens. We will use this image to help discuss some of the key players in our behavior/ responses and you will get a snapshot of how these brain parts function when unaffected by any trauma and then later how it almost feels like a hi-jacking of sorts.

The limbic system (thalamus, hypothalamus, hippocampus, and amygdala) is understood as the emotional and somatosensory memory. It also houses attachment and can perceive and react to threat.

- The thalamus (sits atop the brainstem) directs senses into appropriate areas of the cortex as well as other areas of the brain. Emotions can be very contingent on the things we hear, touch, see, and taste. The sense of smell has its own private relay system that is close to other areas of the brain that regulate emotions so smells can at times have an even more powerful reaction in bringing you back to a certain point in time.
- The hypothalamus plays an incredible role in regulating functions in your body. For emotion, it regulates your autonomic nervous system which we can think of as the fight or flight response vs rest and digest response. It controls the endocrine system and triggers hormones to release into your bloodstream like epinephrine and adrenaline.
- The hippocampus plays a key role in forming new memories and is like your filing cabinet for memory storage. It's critical to converting your short-term memory into long-term memory (Rajmohan & Mohandas, 2007).
- The amygdala helps us detect threat and is involved in stimulating the nervous system to respond to threat. This plays a significant role in fear/anxiety/anger/violence if activated. This is where we store emotionally related memories and the way it typically works is the stronger the emotion, the stronger the memory (McGaugh, 2003). And that goes for whichever the direction of emotion- so you may remember a birthday that stands out more than others because of the intensity in your happiness. And it works the same way when we think of the strong

emotions of fear and anger for example in trauma. Emotion triggered stress hormones make more glucose energy available to fuel brain activity which sends a signal to the brain that something especially important just happened. The amygdala kicks in by initiating a memory trace in the basal ganglia and frontal lobes to boost activity for memory-forming areas (Buchanan, 2007; Kensinger, 2007). The emotional arousal essentially brands certain events into the brain (Brewin et al., 2007).

- A limbic-related part called the anterior insula (not pictured) projects onto the amygdala and is a vital role in joining subjective emotional experiences with interoceptive awareness (means receiving, identifying, accessing, and understanding) of one's body state. It is a part of anticipating aversive stimuli, generalization of fear, and detecting threat.

The prefrontal cortex (not a part of the limbic system) is particularly important in our decision making. Here we have verbal language and analytical reasoning. The frontal cortex has regulatory abilities and houses cognitive functioning. We call this area our executive functioning and you can think of it as the executive board room where decisions are made, and plans are put in place. It has the final say in how to respond to that info that comes in from our thalamus. You can almost imagine a room of people sitting at a table and discussing the information that is presented and how we (the person) should handle it. I can bring a chuckle on with that image now when I have a cognitive mix-up and thinking my staff must be out to lunch.

Here we will walk through these brain parts with a simple example of a group of us sitting outside in the yard for a picnic and a dog walks up (something happens)- the thalamus is going to send that sensory information to the various parts of the brain that are needed to figure out what is happening and then how to respond. Your amygdala and hippocampus are working on sorting through their filing cabinet to help inform the prefrontal cortex. We are taking in several bits of information like if they have a collar on, a leash (which may suggest a friendly neighborhood dog that just got away), is there a person with the dog, does it look like your friend's dog that lives around the corner, is it foaming at the mouth, is the hair standing up (which may signal aggression), etc. That prefrontal cortex then has all that information presented to that board meeting for review plus what it recalls from previous experience and decides to pet it, run from it, give it a snack, yell, or some other response.

Trauma's impact on the brain

Now we will see how that scenario could play out if there was a history of a traumatic dog bite in the past.

The Brain with Past Trauma

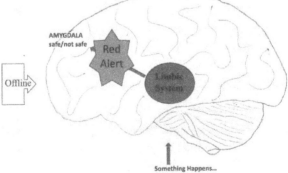

The dog now comes into our yard and the visual cues get relayed to the amygdala (it is like the smoke detector you put in your house- our fire alarm in the brain). It is our emotional memory center and is automatically activated when there is a potential threat or a perception of threat. There's increased activation in the anterior insula to get ready for the threat. So, the Amygdala says, "red alert, alarm" and the prefrontal cortex shuts down, so we are freed up for quicker responding. The emergency stress response system takes over and leaves us disconnected from that board room where we sort and sift through all the information to make rational and logical decisions. Interestingly, this is built in for our benefit- think about the dangers we could face if we had to have a board meeting every time danger may present itself.

The sympathetic nervous system gets activated with a release of adrenaline so that we can have super strength to potentially fight and/or flee. Here we may see an increase in heart rate and respiration, a rush of energy to muscle tissue, that frontal lobe inhibition, and a suppression of non-essential systems (i.e., your digestion would be suppressed so the body can re-route its resources where they are needed).

At some point, the parasympathetic nervous system is triggered to counter the previously mentioned effects. This is our recovery system and is like slamming on the brakes which may cause shaking, trembling, and rebound gastro-intestinal activity. This is also why some patients become nauseous when remembering trauma. It can also result in exhaustion, depletion, shutting down, numbing, and a total collapse. Some people may find it difficult just to get out of bed and the brain does not realize it is over. In that instance of the dog showing up to the picnic, we may immediately run, fight, freeze, or shut down without taking the time to take in all that other informative data that we would have (collar, leash, aggressive behavior).

I then like to connect this to another example that I have seen of a peer coming up to a patient after a lecture to ask a question and without even considering that maybe they just have a question, or a compliment, they react by verbally lashing out at them, quickly escaping to their unit, or freezing in the moment and not being able to speak. They later come back to the unit not having any idea of what just happened, and some may isolate, feel embarrassed, or get irritable.

Trauma survivors may perceive danger faster than others would because of hypervigilance. I bet you can think of situations in which you may have had with loved ones where this seems familiar, where there was a reaction that inevitably leaves both parties with a "whoa where did that even come from?" Or that "hulk-rage" event when your roommate verbally exploded on you for putting the butter back in the wrong spot in the refrigerator. Their use of yelling and carrying on seems grossly out of proportion to you as their roommate. For them, it triggered a recall of feeling like their voice did not matter when they were abused, and they told someone to stop. And now, their placements and organization of items in the kitchen is where they derive some semblance of power and control. It was as if you just stomped on it. These are what we call trauma responses.

Many individuals are not even aware of when and what is happening and then later beat themselves up for it. I have had patients say they felt like something just took over and they couldn't stop it. And if this happened to you as a trauma survivor, you may have even had your partner or friend just add to your own shame and guilt over your behavior, as they may have called you names and told you something is wrong with you. In your rational mind that has some time to reflect on it, you may be recognizing that your roommate had no other intention with that butter than to simply be helpful and clean up after themselves. Or you are like the uninformed roommate in this scenario who didn't understand all that has been going on in this person's world, and without that you resorted to some name-calling that you now wish you could take back. What once served us quite well in helping to protect us though, now has us using a lot of resources and responding in ways that aren't needed, and our brain doesn't quite get it yet.

"Under conditions of extreme stress, there is failure of... memory processing, which results in an inability to integrate incoming data into a coherent autobiographical narrative, leaving the sensory elements of the experience unintegrated and unattached. These sensory elements are then prone to return... when enough of them are activated by current reminders" (Van der Kolk, Hopper, & Osterman 2001 as cited in Fisher 2017). During the threat, the hippocampus (which processes experience prior to its being remembered) is inhibited, and the prefrontal cortex fails to witness the experience. Fisher (2017) teaches that the unprocessed "raw data" of the feelings, sensations, muscle memories, and physical reactions get encoded in the amygdala. This provides a record of what happened yet without a narrative that can explain them or make sense of it. Trauma can shut down the narrative memory which allows the event to get encoded in sensory/implicit memory and the nervous system. It doesn't surprise me when a client doesn't even have a memory or narrative to their story.

Since the amygdala is that "smoke detector" the result is sensitization to even subtle reminders of the traumatic event. "At those moments of feeling under threat, the 'thinking; mind-the frontal cortex- is compromised" (Ogden, 2006, p. 4). Consequently, the behaviors that often follow are impulsive, dangerous, and inappropriate or out of proportion to the individual's current reality. When we are hypo/hyper-aroused, our brain is not functioning properly. The dorsolateral prefrontal cortex, aka the Timekeeper, is not online and is unable to say that "then is THEN, and NOT now." Instead, it is saying "then is now, and I don't know when it is going to end." To a person experiencing a flashback, in the moment it feels like NOW, like it is actually happening now, not back then.

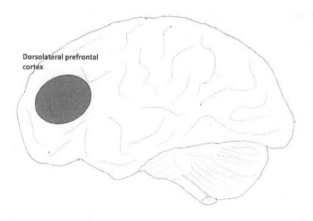

Dorsolateral prefrontal cortex

I have interacted with so many patients who have been so surprised by the psychoeducation around how their experiences of trauma get stored in the body and how it impacts the way the brain responds to events later in life that have nothing to do with the trauma. Our mind and bodies try to work together for our benefit and when that limbic system deems a situation to be unsafe it pulls all forces together to dive into action and help you survive. It is protective in nature yet over time it is as if it goes into full helicopter/hover mode in calling on the protection team too soon with an overreliance on those survival instincts and safeguarding measures. It loses its radar or sense, for what is truly a dangerous situation and can have you reacting in ways that are out of proportion to the situation at hand.

All things considered; you are not to walk away from this page starting to feel shame for the responses that are coming to mind as this starts to resonate with you. And if I could guess, you were already carrying that shame and now you can start giving yourself permission to appreciate and understand how these responses have helped you survive some horrible abuse situations. I like to look at the brain like I would look at how I interact with people. If I have a friend who has been getting overly involved in something in my life, yet they think they have been considering my best interest and I'm not feeling that way, I must have a conversation with them. You might guess that my friend would be less defensive and more open to making a change, when I can show that I appreciate their intent to care for me and be protective. My acknowledging that will make for a much less defensive conversation that can lead to some productive change and strengthening of our relationship. I want that for my brain and me too. As I have one treatment modality coming to mind here, I think about nurturing that part of me that wants to be protective and helping it see that it doesn't have to work as hard anymore.

Making sense of the reactions

This can help us understand how your loved ones can be triggered by a multitude of things that can elicit reactions out of them that may seem out of proportion to the outsider. If you approach a deer in the woods, it may freeze to blend in but if you get too close it will run. Just like in animals, these mechanisms are designed to keep us safe. What can happen though is these responses may get signaled to kick in when you don't need them. If I am in real danger then it is appropriate for my body to respond in kind, the key is getting back on track with differentiating that.

Dr. Banner transforms into the Hulk when he is experiencing moments of anxiety, stress, and anger most of all. In the beginning, he had no control over it, he didn't understand it. Your loved ones may have been living in this reactive experience where they act, feel, and imagine without any recognition of the influence of their past experiences on their present reality. And if they have not had that recognition, I am going to guess a lot of this may be new material for you too in your relationship with them. Emotions can persist without our conscious awareness of what caused them.

One intriguing and relevant experiment was conducted by having individuals with damage to their hippocampus that left them unable to form new explicit memories, view a sad or a happy film. After viewing the films, their emotion of either happiness or sadness persisted, with no recollection of the film they had viewed (Feinstein et al., 2010). Many later say they have no idea why they reacted the way they did. I often reference my friend's book *Eagles Don't Eat Chicken Food* (Boulware-Brown, 2016) in some clinical situations for some great analogies. She discusses how the hindbrain is responsible for housing emotion that is more intricately linked to impulses and reactions that the amygdala is responsible for. "The best part of your skills and abilities are found in the front of your head for a reason and to operate out of emotions is like walking backwards" (p.36).

There are so many things that could potentially trigger one of these responses that has been presented and so much of it depends on the individual so I cannot give you an exhaustive list. That said, therapy itself can be triggering. And for anyone who is a counseling student reading this or a beginning clinician please take note- Do NOT ask your clients and patients to trust you. Just pause here for a second and try to make sense of that without any explanation from me. I can wait. …….. How many individuals have been violated by others who have said "just trust me"?

At times, the therapeutic role can start off with uncertainty, a power differential (perceived or indeed and unfortunately exploited as one), fear, and some clinicians may not have enough knowledge and experience to set up a safe space. And even those who do have that competence and who put every effort into providing that supportive environment may still need the reminder that the client has their own internal experience around the issue of safety to consider. Sometimes the mention of a safe space can feel unsafe. The word *body* may need to be switched out by saying something like "what do you feel *inside* right now?" Of course, the more obvious is that certain people, places, and things may elicit a response, or being ignored, facing intimacy, being put on the spot, and feeling in the middle of conflict. Emotions, vulnerability, eye contact, authority figures, loud noises, and finding oneself in a committed relationship are just a few other examples of potential triggers.

Trauma survivors have symptoms as we understand it in our field instead of what most think of it as being memories (Harvey, 1990). These symptoms represent how that person survived and how the body adapted to the enormity of the abnormal conditions. Many people view trauma as less about what happened and more about how our bodies have stored it. Bessel van der Kolk's (2014) book *The Body Keeps the Score* provides a jam-packed, in-depth look into this process, offering up a wealth of research and scientific advances if anyone should want to further their reading.

Even for us clinicians in the field we know that we are often bumping up against behaviors or anger, self-injury, anxiety, and shutting down just to name a few. For a visual, think of sitting in a chair classroom style, yet there are just two there. The chair in the front are those behaviors that may be protecting what is sitting in the chair behind, the fear, the vulnerability, the feeling of not being in control, and I must be curious about that back chair when the front one is staring me in the face. We don't get very far if we try to bulldoze the stuff that is in the front chair protecting the chair that is holding the trauma. Why would the back chair even want to let us in? How we treat the front chair's behavior influences if we get let in as the protector parts can get activated.

Many people don't recognize or identify their symptoms as serving a purpose, they just have a reaction to them, and often a negative one. I was always taught to be curious about the function of certain behaviors and symptoms. Depression for example may have helped the person survive by creating a sense that no one can get to them if they shut down like they are in a cave. And so closely tied to that is a decreased interest in things or activities they used to enjoy. If I am no longer interested, then it won't hurt when it is taken away from me. Irritability is great at helping to push people away to avoid getting hurt. And numbing, well that allows me to not have to feel the pain. Starting to ring a bell?

Yet, the fallout comes, and one begins to see how something that has once had a purpose in helping them survive is now creating more of a cost for them. Your loved ones are now gaining awareness and learning new skills. Albeit they are a bit scary. And oftentimes, we see this take time because although it may make perfect sense to the observer, what is new and healthy in terms of new behaviors and actions, can be very scary to the individual. What is old and unhealthy is familiar to them and thus comfortable.

SECTION 4

Trauma's Relationship with Addiction

I f we remember some of that development mentioned earlier, it is not uncommon for individuals who have had a prolonged period of chronic victimization to experience difficulties with emotional regulation. Children begin to learn to self-soothe exceedingly early on in infancy and many have established some solid skills by about 6 months of age. Yet, for those children experiencing trauma early on, they are not taught appropriate ways to regulate their emotions or manage their physical arousal. And with this we can see coping mechanisms that have developed like self-injurious behavior (i.e., cutting and burning their skin), substance use, and disordered eating behaviors. And other high-risk behaviors and suicide attempts may have become short term (even though potentially permanent) solutions to overwhelming emotional distress.

Some behaviors that others may label as aggressive or acting out may be more helpfully reframed as attempts at problem solving in the face of painful emotions, so that we don't lose our empathy now that we understand it better. For someone with complex/developmental trauma their responses become more of survival versus exploration. As a child your whole purpose is to explore and be little scientists, but instead, due to everything going on the child goes into survival mode and this means they are not taking in all the things they ordinarily would to teach them about other people, the self, and the world. Thus, as they get older, they do not know how to judge their world.

A substantial portion of those who live with a substance use disorder have reported a history of abuse as a child. Holding that information in mind, one may reframe the war on drugs as a war on traumatized people who need help. Many people turn to substance use to self-medicate and avoid the mood symptoms that come with trauma. The painful experiences and negative comments that were once said to them play repeatedly in their head. Patients tell me they use substances as a coping mechanism; it became the solution. In substance use disorder treatment, we teach that avoidance gives power to the feelings and thoughts being avoided. When you try to lock the pain away, it might be out of sight, but it is not out of mind. Using substances to disconnect from the pain does not change the reality that those experiences still happened. Eventually, if left unaddressed, it impacts the way you relate to yourself and others. A good portion of those with PTSD also have a substance use disorder (SUD) and integrated and simultaneous treatment is necessary.

Window of tolerance is a term coined by Dr. Dan Siegel (1999) and refers to the optimal arousal zone where one can tolerate the ebb and flow of a range of emotions, to regulate their emotional state even when under stress, and to self-soothe. We can build an array of strategies and internal resources to help us stay in this zone. Substance use can precede trauma experiences and symptoms. For those who identify their substance use as a coping mechanism or a survival strategy, it makes sense if the aim is to numb hyperarousal symptoms like impulsivity and reactivity. Or it can be a self-medication for hypoarousal symptoms of depression, maybe it helps block out intrusive recall, or quiet painful emotions and thoughts. For some it can stimulate when needing to come out of a numb experience, or it can induce relaxation from being overstimulated. This all depends obviously on the type of substances used.

When trauma and addiction are related for an individual, sobriety alone is insufficient as the absence of their substance may allow for a flooding of emotions, recall, and flashbacks which then in turn predispose them to using again. Using a substance again after a period of sobriety can be an impulsive panic attempt to restore the false window of tolerance. Remember, Brickel (2020) shared how substance use (and the other self-injurious behaviors noted above) can be a dissociative mechanism to escape their feelings. Oftentimes individuals present to substance use treatment and say they are ready to get sober, yet not ready to work on their trauma. Or we even see some treatment providers put focus on getting sober first before working on trauma. And less often we may still see a provider encourage treatment for the trauma before working on the substance use. But more times than not we have to face the reality that recovering from either of those often requires one to recover from both, and simultaneously.

Traditional sequential and segregated treatment models, where patients were expected to get substance use treatment first and then focus on trauma, presents several challenges to patients and treatment providers, and may unintentionally contribute to the poorer prognosis observed in individuals with co-occurring PTSD-SUD. Integrated treatments focusing on both trauma and substance use concurrently, allow for a reciprocal experience of symptom reduction and improvement. Patients educated about self-medication and coping by use of substances, explore the costs and benefits, and develop alternative effective methods.

Substance use disorders and mental health diagnoses for a long-time have come with a high burden of stigma and fear of judgment, despite the facts around the prevalence of both in millions of homes just in the United States alone. There are a lot of inaccurate beliefs and misunderstanding about substance use and mental health in the public which can lessen the likelihood of some individuals seeking help when they need it or to continue with treatment once enrolled. Even our language in how we refer to these individuals, both in the public domain with family and friends as well as in the therapeutic community, plays a significant role in the stigma. Using person first language by referring to someone as a person who has a substance use disorder vs a "drug abuser" or "addict" can shift the lens to a person who has a problem that can be addressed, rather than the person being the problem.

We also need to realize or recognize how much judgment and shame can live within our own field, not just in the public domain. One of my most dreaded quotes I have heard for years has to do with knowing an "addict" is lying because their mouth is moving. I have heard it repeated by peers going through substance use treatment, or who have been maintaining sobriety, and have heard it passed around between clinicians in so many different settings both clinical and academic. The problem with that is the implication that these individuals lie all the time. And then what is the point of working on their trustworthiness with others if they will always be labeled that way. I also like to encourage us to be more curious about what drives lies in the first place- protection. From what? People at all ages can tell a lie out of efforts in protection. Maybe its protection from a consequence, but I would guess that when speaking specifically about the people we serve in our field, it has more to do with attempts to ward off judgment, shame, and embarrassment. We need to explore what our role (clinicians, family, friends) may be in the situation. Am I giving off vibes that it is not safe to be vulnerable and honest with me?

SECTION 5

What About Collective Trauma?

C ollective trauma refers to the psychological impact of traumatic experiences on entire groups of people, communities, or societies. There are several major events that people can witness/experience as a large group that can affect how people act, think, and feel and these can include wars, terrorism, natural disasters, economic disasters, mass violence, and pandemics. Yes, I said pandemics and it can have long term effects. And during the COVID-19 pandemic we also experienced other collective trauma on top of it including several of those mentioned above- natural disasters, economic disasters, and multiple mass shootings. At the time of my final editing, we just came through an interrupted attempt to riot at a Pride event for the LGBTQ+ community as well as mass shootings at a medical facility, an elementary school, and one at a grocery store that was racially motivated. And let me not minimize, as a community can be impacted even with one fatality. We have also had the pandemic toppled with broadcastings for all to view that further illuminated long-standing racial injustice. This type of trauma can affect entire communities and alter relationships, health, policies, and social norms.

Collective trauma can result in psychological distress and a trans-generational burden. There are several collective traumatic events in our history that have resulted in increased suicide rates, depression, anxiety, PTSD, and have an overall impact on one's general mental well-being. The impact of collective trauma at the societal level can include damaged national pride, increased individual and collective fear, feelings of humiliation, identity crisis, increased feelings of vulnerability, and heightened vigilance for new threats. People in this pandemic may be questioning their future existence as an individual and as a society. And although we may have been weathering the same storm, we are not all in the same boat in terms of access to resources and support or premorbid status that may be systemically influenced.

We also have collective memories that get passed down to future generations contributing to trans-generational/intergenerational effects on future descendants. Dr. Rachel Yehuda has done work in the area, helping us understand how both trauma and resilience cross generations. We know that "Holocaust offspring were more likely to have PTSD, depression and anxiety if they had a parent with PTSD" and Yehuda (2021) shares "many of the mental health effects of intergenerational trauma, I think, are a consequence of parental symptoms, and not their exposure, per se." Our brains and bodies can inherit the impact of trauma in the way we express genes. And we can learn from what is modeled out of their behaviors and symptoms. Think of someone who lived through the Great Depression for example whose children were impacted by their experience and shifts in planning, spending, and the like, out of fear. We also can see panic, grief, anger, and hopelessness surface and become chronic. Researchers published a rapid review in the *Lancet* (Zhang, et. al., 2020) and noted that isolation and quarantine contributed to several negative psychological effects including anger, PTSD, and confusion. I know I have seen this in patients as a contributing factor to their substance use and increase in mental health issues as an example.

COVID-19 has forced us to explore, question, and understand how governments protect people, which involves engaging a level of trust when we are unsure of who to trust- trust in rules, orders, restrictions, mask wearing, science, and that someone out there has our personal best interest in mind. It has shifted what going to school looks and feels like, what threat and danger look like, and our understanding of society and other people. Remember that man I mentioned way back- Erik Erikson, and how he posed that we develop a sense of trust in our first year of life that comes out of an experience as infants that we can trust the people around us and that the world is generally a predictable place. He found it to be so fundamental to our continued existence into adulthood and out of that development of trust we obtain a sense of hope and optimism. The key event at that phase of life is feeding; a pandemic serves to disrupt this existence of hope and predictability of our world on so many levels, and for many it has come full circle back to that feeding as people were now faced with uncertainty of even their basic survival needs getting met.

The pandemic alone (although we know we have those other collective traumatic experiences added to it) has disrupted our dreams and impeded our plans- from vacation and travel, to key rites of passage and milestones that may have included celebrating graduations, weddings, birthdays; athletic goals we had been training and working towards; prom/homecoming; and moving out on one's own to start school, a new job, or a new business. It may have hampered our sense of mission, pursuit, and goals that give us strength and motivation. It hijacked our place in the world as it took away jobs, our favorite hobbies/activities/restaurants, and stole our contact with people who help us feel a sense of belonging and love.

We were unable to be physically close to loved ones, lost loved ones- and hadn't even been able to honor their life and passing with traditional ceremonies of honor and memorializing. There are the harrowing experiences of healthcare professionals who cared for COVID-19 patients and dealt with death day after day with no relief and carrying the weight of being the last person that patient got to see as loved ones were unable to say goodbye. Many felt like they lost those significant social touchpoints they often enjoy with others, which liven up our days and give us some confidence that we matter to them and to this world. And others may have been pushed into isolation and confinement that was unsafe. Children going through abuse at home may have lost the safe space of their school setting that gave them solace for eight hours of the day. Domestic violence among partners also did not take a break during the pandemic, and if anything, increased. The subsequent PTSD that can result from these experiences in recent months should not be minimized.

Someone's experience in the COVID-19 pandemic, back-to-school uncertainty, rising unemployment rates, and the events and aftermath of political discord and significant issues and events in our social climate in and of themselves may have been traumatic. And, in some cases, the emotions people experienced were more than just a reaction to today's troubling times. For some, their anxiety and fear are rooted in unresolved past trauma or current trauma due to loss or extreme circumstances. This pandemic may have dug up some adverse events or feelings from their past. For example, if a person experienced a sexual assault, the feelings around trust, control, self-esteem, and safety brought up by the pandemic could contribute to a more intense experience of powerlessness.

The signs can be subtle, and people are often not thinking consciously about the trauma at the root of their behavior. They may have memories of a trauma that happened when they were 13, but they may not realize on a conscious level their response to the pandemic was triggering those prior emotions and experiences. That individual may perceive she is anxious because of back-to-school uncertainty, but when we take a closer look at her symptoms in a self-assessment, it becomes clear there is a connection to the past that must be addressed to help resolve her current symptoms.

We also have social psychology terms to consider around the topic of attribution and determining the cause of behavior. One may act from the fundamental attribution error (Ross, 1977), which is the tendency to overestimate the dispositional causes of behaviors and to underestimate the external causes. What does that mean in plain language? Dispositional refers to the internal and stable factors like their ability, intelligence, personality, and character. The external causes refer to the social situation, physical environment, or the characteristics of the task at hand. This would be attributing the rude behavior of the person you encountered to who they are at their core, the kind of person they are, rather than possibility and empathy of them having a difficult day or just receiving some unwelcome news.

There is also a tendency to turn to situational factors when it comes to one's own behavior to rationalize or excuse away but targeting someone else's character when looking at their actions. A student who did not complete their homework may be looked at as lazy, irresponsible, and unconcerned with their future. Perhaps they are experiencing some chaos at home right now or had a major loss that is throwing off their focus and concentration.

The ultimate attribution error (Pettigrew, 1979) is when one ascribes the cause of a behavior to what may be seen as dispositional characteristics of a particular group of people, instead of the individual themselves. An example is: a woman exhibits some behavior and then it is looked at as "see, its because she is a woman." And we can replace *woman* with lesbian, Muslim, African American, etc. A stereotype is a generalization about an individual or a group based on their categorization. Some say there are positive stereotypes, and I will challenge that a bit because the person making the comment may think it is positive, yet does the recipient? What if they do not fit that stereotype accurately, does it say something about them if they are Asian and get poor grades? They put people in boxes for our convenience, so we do not have to take the time to fully analyze a situation. And could a "positive" stereotype of one group naturally imply something less than for another group? I think we need to take all of this into consideration when interacting with others.

Think about the impact on students who went through virtual schooling (at all levels) along with the many individuals who had to shift their work environment to virtual settings. People experience fatigue from virtual platforms and overuse of video conferencing and the consequences that follow. This is a challenge for educators as they are just as impacted, and then facilitating it for their students.

There are health issues that come with too much screen time that can include aches and pains in one's neck, arms, lower back, and tired eyes. I have also spoken with optometrists who have anecdotally shared that they have a lot of patients complaining about headaches. I can share a personal example of my son needing glasses in the first fall of the COVID-19 pandemic after his virtual schooling experience left him with debilitating headaches from all the blue light exposure. Students were spending several hours a day in virtual learning, and this is in addition to working online on reports and research. Now we add in the synchronous and even asynchronous content (if the lectures are recorded for online viewing at their convenience).

Dr. Brenda Widerhold, a clinical psychologist, commented that communication over virtual platforms is not in fact real-time (Walker, 2020). "Our brains are used to pick up body language and other cues, not to mention increases of dopamine that are experienced during face-to-face communication. On a video call, something is off, and our subconscious brain is reacting to it. Communication isn't in real time, even though we may think it is." This is in reference to the lag time, even a millisecond delay, which can trigger the brain to look for ways to overcome that lack of synchrony, leaving it to fatigue and have us feeling tired, anxious, and worried. In social interaction we rely heavily on non-verbal cues, micro-expressions, body language, etc. that are more evident in a classroom setting. Surprisingly for some, most of our communication is non-verbal. Thus, we can miss important signals and it impacts us as educators in our ability to read a room.

Another issue with the framed face and not getting the rest of the nonverbal cues, is the person can appear large on the monitor and those larger faces can ignite the fight or flight response which allows cortisol to flow and rev up your stress response. Every time we get into this activation of our sympathetic nervous system, we then need our parasympathetic nervous system to employ to pump the breaks. When we go through this frequently because of extreme or prolonged stress (which can sum up 2020-2022 for many) it can leave us with a diminished ability to perform at our typical capacity. Aside from physical and mental health symptoms, it can leave us disinterested in our work, restless, tense, forgetful, and having concentration difficulties. As a professor myself, I can say I have had an influx of emails from students explaining forgetfulness and asking for grace in turning in late assignments, as well as some self-disclosure from the students of how this experience is bringing out lower grades.

And then there is a thing of chatter and communication that often spontaneously show up after a class lecture held in person where students walk up and ask the professor questions after class. This can be for clarification of concepts and assignments, or just interest and insight that was sparked by something said during class. Students do not often stay after class virtually to talk any further as exhaustion has set in. This in and of itself can leave them feeling less connected to their educators.

Maladaptive behaviors can result from all of this like self-injury, substance use, acting out, or withdrawing as many lack the resources or coping skills to respond. For many of our students, academics is part of that journey of finding their purpose and seeing their value, so especially with the uncertainty that is out there right now, we want to help students continue to be successful in their courses so they can reinstate some sort of hope and predictability in their lives again. With an unseen potentially deadly virus around, our smoke detector- the amygdala, is on constant alert and leading to higher levels of anxiety. While I have not treated anyone yet who has had a trauma diagnosis stemming from direct experience with COVID-19, I imagine several months from now we may start seeing those individuals just as we did in the aftermath of 9/11. There is no doubt we will continue to deal with the emotional after-effects of the pandemic for years. We want to validate people's experiences and encourage them to address their trauma before it causes greater physical or emotional harm.

SECTION 6

Trauma Related to Race/Identity/Culture

E xperiences related to racism, discrimination, and microaggressions compounded the collective trauma of the pandemic for many. We had a concurrent racial justice movement and racial reckoning following instances of police violence against people of color and the murder of George Floyd, which brought to the forefront issues of racism and racial injustice that have been longstanding in our society.

Let me first differentiate that a stereotype is a cognitive categorization/generalization; prejudice is a negative judgment about a member based on their categorization (it is evaluative in nature); and discrimination is a negative behavior based on their categorization and is an action. There are individuals who shy away and encourage we leave behind our history but if we do not validate the impact it has on groups of people and fail to challenge and correct the falsehoods and inaccurate beliefs that drove it, then we stand to repeat it, and that is what has been happening.

Many individuals that I hear get outraged in responding to claims of racism associate it with blatant and over acts or hate crimes. Now, this has been illuminated simultaneously with the pandemic. And aside from those more obvious situations, a lot of racism has evolved into a more subtle and ambiguous form. It has gone underground a bit, better disguised or excused away by something else, and is more likely to be covert. I have had conversations with other White individuals for example that are quick to get defensive about racist acts/beliefs. And often these are from an unconscious bias and are unintentional. Yet due to that, have the potential to do actual harm because we are not in full awareness of what is driving our responses in situations. Yes, everyone carries bias and prejudice. Privilege and racism are a different story.

Racism involves a systemic advantage that is based on race. And Beverly Daniel Tatum (2017) points out, "And, equally important, there is no systematic cultural and institutional support or sanction for the racial bigotry of people of color." And privilege has nothing to with socioeconomic status. I recall not long after Trayvon Martin was killed, a triple digit millionaire celebrity speaking about getting stopped by security in his own building of residence (owned the penthouse) as he got off the elevator because someone else who was in the elevator with him was suspicious of his look for being a Black man wearing a hoodie. What I mean by that is someone can be White and poor and walk into a store and not be followed around with the belief that they may steal something. The staff don't know that they cannot afford what is in the store or that they work their butt off to make below poverty but being White makes them less suspicious.

In that scenario, we see skin color; we don't see their bank accounts. People have challenges in life and obstacles to face, yet the concept of White privilege just emphasizes that skin color is not one of those contributing factors to life being harder. I believe this is where the difference in messaging is.

Intention

Being unaware of committing an insensitive act or comment lends itself to defending intent rather than content. I had a parent once say to me after I requested a conversation around a racist comment that was said to my daughter in kindergarten (my children are biracial and this was only the first incident for her, others have already come) that her son could not have meant any harm by it and that he must have been referring to something else. Dr. Ken Hardy (2015) poses that "pure intentions can render impure consequences." He explains that the argument of intentionality often arises, yet that is designed more to take care of the person who made the remark, it is not on behalf of the relationship. If I closed my child's arm in the door on accident, it is not helpful if I go on a defensive rant about how much I did not mean to do it, or how they should not have been standing there in the doorway as they were. In all of that, I am not tending to her hurt arm.

The parent added that her family does not teach their kids to be racist and in fact, teaches their children to be color-blind and to see everyone the same. For anyone who understands this topic well, I know right there you just paused with a full-body reaction. First, let me clarify something- you are not in the clear just because you aren't teaching your kids to be racist, we need to teach our children to NOT be racist (or anti-racist). Otherwise, they can fall right in line with comments and actions that come from racism because they weren't taught to recognize it as such.

The same applies to teaching our children NOT to be prejudiced. Our children are watching us, they watch what we say, and they watch our non-verbal too. And they look at who we associate with. If you don't have any friends or family who are a race, religion, ethnicity, or sexuality different from your own, you don't get a pass of having to have these conversations about differences. If anything, you have even more reason to have them, to teach against the messages they may be making up in their own minds, or the messages they will pick up from others (thus leading them to anti-discrimination). If you say "stop staring" when your child sees someone with a prosthetic or in a wheelchair, you miss an opportunity to chat about differences. Remember, children are scientists, and they will make meaning out of things. Avoiding conversations about diversity could lead them to believe you have negative views on a particular topic or group. They will reason in their own head about why you aren't discussing it. You may be an ally to a variety of groups, but especially if they may not see those individuals in your circle in life, they won't know it if you aren't speaking about it with them. They can probably handle a lot more in conversation than you think.

Back to being blind, I think we also bring in wanting to be neutral. This makes me think of one of my favorite quotes of all time by Bishop Desmond Tutu, "If you are neutral in situations of injustice, you have chosen the side of the oppressor. If an elephant has its foot on the tail of a mouse and you say that you are neutral, the mouse will not appreciate your neutrality." And what some do not understand is that being color-blind is one of the cardinal sins of multiculturalism. And I think for those who are not well versed in this topic, here is a place to start, as we don't always know what we don't know.

In my teen years I used the same term for myself and thought it was good; it was well-intentioned, yet I did not understand the potential implications at the time. Being blind to the obvious differences in skin color allow one to ignore and invalidate the experiences of that person. If I see everyone the same, then I am looking at it through my lens and what I experience as someone who identifies as White, therein potentially minimizing challenges, obstacles, and overt racism that a person of color may experience.

If I am color-blind then I cannot understand why my husband, who identifies as Black, keeps his registration and license above his visor in the car. With that ignorance I don't see his fear of getting shot for reaching in his glove box if pulled over, due to implicit bias. Seeing that his experience is not the same as mine allows me to have empathy, albeit fear when he has called my phone while getting pulled over just to hear what happens- just in case.

Seeing our differences can be fruitful as that empathy for each other's experience grows, allows us to be better allies, and teaches us about our world rather than through a lens of sameness. Some refer to different geographic locations in the United States as melting pots, yet that may mean losing identities. I like to take an approach more of fostering appreciation for differences and uniqueness. This may seem like trivial language shift to some, but it holds such powerful implications for our viewpoints. And remember, true empathy is really imagining what it is like to be in someone else's experience. But I must do this while also imagining their life experiences up to that point as well, because without that, then I see their current situation through my lens that is shaped by my past and current situation. Consequently, that results in me still not being able to imagine myself in their shoes fully.

Race-based trauma can result from major experiences of racism, or it can be the result of an accumulation of many small occurrences, such as the buildup of everyday micro-aggressions. This has been a hot topic over the last several years and I have been teaching about micro-aggressions over the past 15 to my undergraduate and graduate students. They "are the everyday slights, put-downs, invalidations, and insults directed to socially devalued group members by well-intentioned people who often are unaware that they have engaged in such biased and harmful behaviors (Sue & Sue, 2019, p.12)."

There is a fantastic video on YouTube (Fusion, 2016) comparing microaggressions to mosquito bites. I highly recommend you pause here and look it up as it makes it easily digestible. These can be subtle, verbal, non-verbal, and can affect physical and mental health over time. They are often hard to prove because people have alternative explanations as to what they were referring to. Many of them are automatic and a product of society and everything else individuals are exposed to in their upbringing.

Sue and Sue (2019) describe several types of micro-aggressions with the first two typically outside of conscious awareness and unintentional. A microinsult is when someone delivers a verbal statement that conveys rudeness or insensitivity. Getting complimented for speaking well or something like "you aren't like the rest" has an insulting message even if not intended. It can be someone of multiracial identity getting remarks like "you don't look mixed" or being asked to ascribe to one race (which is known as hypodescent). I can remember when my son was getting registered with a new pediatrician and was asked what race he identified with. I said he is biracial, and we argued back and forth as she pressured me to pick one. I said I didn't care what was on her paper for her to pick, she can write in my response.

My field is still challenged with becoming more intentionally inclusive in asking a married person the name of their spouse or partner, and not using the language that assumes the relationship is heterosexual. Maybe the microinsult is felt when you give an eyebrow raise or a "wow" response for a woman in leadership out of surprise because you expected the boss to be a man, or when you are interviewing candidates for a job and look surprised when they arrive to your office, and it does not match the race or ethnicity that you imagined the name to be attached to. A couple colleagues and I have a research publication in the National Social Science journal (McDonough, et al., 2020) that supports how even a name can impact the attributions we make which affects us in education, housing applications, bank loans, etc. even before the person is physically seen. You can watch a video on YouTube (2014) about how Jose' Zamora dropped the 's' from his name after getting rejected on applications, and how that one small moved changed it all.

A microinvalidation is an unintentional verbal comment or behavior that dismisses the thoughts, feelings, or realities of a target person. Again, these are outside the level of conscious awareness most times, but at times may be in some level of awareness yet used to avoid a difficult or uncomfortable conversation. An example could be when someone tells you that they feel they were on the receiving end of prejudice, discrimination, or some unfair situation and your response may be that "you are being too sensitive," "just get thicker skin," "you are reading too much into it," or one step further in insinuating responsibility on the person in front of you by saying "maybe it was your tone" to justify the reaction. This is even done in the therapy office unfortunately, which is one influence on why our premature termination rate for clients from marginalized groups is almost double that of White clients.

The third type is different in that it is intentional. Most of the time for someone to engage in a microassault there needs to be a situation with some anonymity, an environment where others share your belief, and where the person loses control or becomes disinhibited. A microassault is a blatant attack of a discriminatory nature or conveying bias. Because these are clear when it comes to the intention, it is posed by some that they are easier to deal with than other types only due to knowing where one stands and having less to figure out on how to perceive what just happened. The first two types mentioned often leave people questioning where here the message is clear.

The media coverage of the murders of George Floyd and Ahmaud Arbery, just to reference two, was instrumental in getting justice yet juxtaposed with another trauma for many who witnessed it. There have been racially motivated killings that have been streamed live which allows the trauma to further permeate. The media exposure helps hold people accountable, and at the same time traumatizes those who watch. These images cannot be erased. There's been a lot of talk in the field around the impact on children of color from viewing it and impacting their overall outlook.

Experiences with racial discrimination are linked with negative health outcomes and are the strongest for Black Americans (Carter, 2007). This can include physical pain, cardiovascular issues, hypertension, and calcification of arteries just to name a few. Added to that could be depression, anxiety, trauma related diagnoses, and hopelessness. And children are affected by what they saw and continue to see. Two years later, I turned around in the car one day to find my daughter streaming tears down her face; she was picturing the image of George Floyd lying on the ground with his neck being knelt on... two years later.

During the pandemic we also saw hate crimes increase for Asian-Americans driven by divisive xenophobic rhetoric and blaming a virus on a whole group of people. Many Asian Americans experienced threats, discrimination, violence, and social isolation during the pandemic. Naturally, there is a mental health impact from this in a community that already has some reluctance to seek medical care. We see a variety of marginalized groups be trepidatious in seeking mental health services, not just because of ways that the therapeutic community has oppressively contributed historically, but still today with bias and imposing values and standards on others and misunderstanding a variety of multicultural issues.

Oppression is not new to us, and what many shutter to acknowledge is that this country has built on it and shaped it since its founding. For those who may be ready to interrupt and question me, being a proud American and recognizing the impact of how things once were and how it continues to affect others are not mutually exclusive. You can see it all for what it is and want to make things better. Tatum's book (2017) is a favorite reference of mine for my multicultural courses and gives a fitting example for those who often have responses like- "I didn't ask to be treated with more privilege," or "I didn't own slaves". She shares a scenario of housing discrimination which we know still happens, where the person of color gets denied an apartment, leaving it open for a White tenant. This White tenant benefits from racism and although unsuspecting/unknowing and not to blame for the prior discrimination, still benefits from it anyway.

Experiences with racism do not affect mental health only, there are long-standing physical health implications. Race, as a social construct, gives way to different early life conditions, which may induce epigenetic changes that sustain racial differences in chronic pain. Yes, I said race is a social construct and there are some great documentaries (i.e., Race: The power of an illusion, 2003) and books where you can learn the real history of why it was created. And such an arbitrary concept, to where you may be identified as one race in a particular state, yet crossing lines into another state it changed, has potentially lethal consequences.

Dr. Robert Carter coined the term Race-Based Traumatic Stress Injury as a non-pathological concept that better captures the issue being with external and structural systems rather than a problem with their character. The core stressor of this type of trauma is emotional pain rather than a threat to one's life, although this can certainly be the case in overt acts and distinguishes this traumatic stress from PTSD.

When I think about all that has come out in the last couple years around the immigration process and undocumented individuals, first and foremost the conversation should employ a dialogue that promotes respect and human dignity. And unless you are of Indigenous ancestry, be careful before tackling the topic of rightful passage and citizenship. I did not do anything special to earn the right to be an American except having the fortune of my parents being on this soil before me. A student doing a presentation in one of my classes a few years back brought out a sample citizenship test to see who could pass it. It proved a good point.

And this ties right back into that fundamental attribution error you just learned about. This tendency has left our society in a very judgmental place at times, often invalidating others' experiences, struggles, journeys, and obstacles. I have often heard comments that people who do not have a job, get food stamps, or receive welfare are lazy and want to loaf off others socially. Sure, I imagine there may be some individuals like this of any race or ethnicity, but I would venture a guess that more of them are not happy with their situation and would rather be working for more income than they are receiving and a chance at a sense of purpose and fulfillment. People are less often to point the blame at lack of jobs, an unexpected layoff, an illness, and discrimination just to name a few. And with transparency, I can speak from first-hand experience that my reliance on multiple assistances with a newborn baby and my husband finding a new job as we moved to a new state, while on my pre-doctoral internship (many years ago) that paid below the poverty line, was not laziness. A Place at the Table (2013) is a documentary I share in class that can really shift your perspective on those who receive social services.

SECTION 7

Emotions Revisited

D isney Pixar's film *Inside Out* being labeled in the Family/ Comedy genre is on point as it is not just for children's entertainment (my opinion of course). It has a lot of influence as a learning tool for any age of how important it is to not only have emotions, but to recognize them, lean into them, and let them serve us. I have seen countless patients who have been fearful of letting themselves acknowledge and feel certain emotions as if the consequence was a complete and total unraveling to which there was no return. And we cannot just run from emotions or try to bury them; let us think about this for a second in plain terms- just because you bury something doesn't make it dead.

Additionally, we don't want to de-sensitize people from feeling their emotions because it affects all feelings in general. When one starts to run at the site of emotion, or shut down, they miss out on experiencing other emotions. In addition, trying to live with happiness in the driver seat at all times is not only unrealistic but it's also not healthy. Sometimes leaning into sadness and having care and concern for one's inner self is all the nurturance that is needed to be able to take the next step, go about your day, or one step further to allow healing to take place.

There is a societal and cultural influence on this as well in that we are taught to only present what is going well in our lives. One can look at social media to see how much of our world is posting all the good stuff that we want others to see, living in a front, a façade, and being fearful of what others will think if they see our vulnerabilities and the stuff that is not so hot in our lives right now. Think of the filters used and the planning of what to capture, positioning, and the re-takes. As Mary J. Blige's lyrics in *Roses* (2007) state that "it ain't all roses, flowers and posin'" yet we forget this ourselves when we live in comparison and contrast of everyone else that we look at.

How many of you have been told things like showing your emotions is a sign of weakness? Women are often looked at as ineffective in leadership because of being emotional. What does that even mean? And are we all the same? And let us not ignore that the gender stereotype itself implies men do not and should not have emotions. We all have emotions, and I am thankful for it. I know some of you wish you could block out what some may refer to as the bad emotions or the painful ones. I take issue with us continuing to divide emotions into categories of good and bad, or positive and negative. That labeling itself only serves to butt heads with trying to provoke a shift in our culture. If I see something as negative, I may run from it too, or feel less than or cheated for having to experience it. Our beliefs about our emotions matter, and it can even shape what you end up doing with those emotions. They provide us with useful data about what is happening around us. Anger, sadness, fear? Would you like to block those out?

Unfortunately, many have learned the hard way in trying to avoid specific emotions, that it ends up cutting you off from others that you want to encounter. Anyone of you who has ever tried to numb out the undesired emotions with substances eventually learns that it keeps you from those you desire too. We don't have a switch that can turn a particular category of emotions off and leave another category on. The Serenity Prayer so often referenced in addiction treatment can lend itself to any domain as it asks, "God grant me the serenity to accept the things I cannot change, courage to change the things I can, and wisdom to know the difference." And in this case, there is power to change the way we view emotions, the way we let them say something about us for having or expressing them. It is about the internal dialogue we have with them. We will come back to the issue of reframing our thoughts later. But even if there were a switch to turn a certain set off, knowing what I know now, I just hope someone would cover it with tape.

Pure raw emotion only lasts seconds unless something is keeping it going- a thought. One thought carries into another, and another, and then a thought train pulls out of the gate with your sanity and logical mind. Sometimes when emotions come into the body we go into our head and think. Some of that that is out of distraction and avoidance and being out of touch with our physical/physiological experiences. Sometimes the mind tells us not to feel the body. Practicing mindfulness (being present) we can stop being afraid of our feelings and then stop avoiding them, stop avoiding the things that bring them on, and stop engaging in the unhealthy behaviors that take them away i.e., gadgets, drugs, sexual behavior.

Our emotions serve a purpose and luckily, they can also prepare us for action, or provide direction. Think about anger for a minute, this alerts you to a boundary violation taking place that needs addressing. It pushes you to confront the person or the situation that is involved in your annoyance or irritability, or even confront your own thought process. Think about anger underlying a fight for justice and fairness and mobilizing others for support. Anger is a natural response to a threat and can help us defend ourselves; it can fuel our strength. We need a dose of this for survival and yes, with consideration to healthy delivery and expression of it depending on the situation. I know I referenced my friend's quote earlier about not leading with emotion because of it being like walking backwards, so yes, we do have to have a relationship between our executive board room and the limbic system. Emotions can create colossal damage when poorly expressed. Even so, we can still learn from them and thanks to our brain's neuroplasticity we can create new neural pathways, new patterns of responding. But the more we fear our emotions, the more we allow them to control us.

The wonderful thing is that imperfection is what makes us human. Hulk ran away with shame and embarrassment over his limbic system running wild and then he became afraid to express any anger for fear of what he may do. He learned he no longer had to lock himself up and that he could find that balance. I once had a patient share that she was so afraid of letting herself even feel her anger, let alone express it, because she was certain that once it was unleashed there would be no end. Her counselor and I worked with her together on this and the patient was able to see it sort of like an unraveling piece of clothing- at some point it stops. And she and her counselor were able to joke about not bursting into flames and it encouraged her to start recognizing and giving the attention her emotions deserved.

The character Sadness in *Inside Out* (spoiler alert) turns out to be the hero in the end by tapping into Riley's memories that are filled with family love and support as she is currently dealing with feelings of loss around her life as it was. You may know some folks who are a bit like the character of Joy who try to avoid any acknowledgment of other emotions outside of that happiness, let alone any outward expression of it. But Sadness surprises Joy in a couple of scenes at how important it is to allow these other emotions to sit in the front seat for a bit.

There is a clip that I often show in one of my psychoeducational groups with patients where Joy and Sadness are being guided by Riley's old imaginary friend Bing Bong to the core memories. Bing Bong becomes sad and starts crying in reminiscing about the days when Riley and he would play together. Joy is surprised when her efforts at cheering him up are beaten out by Sadness leaning into the feeling and the conversation. She is dumbfounded at the result (watch the film!). Joy learns so much about how other emotions help us connect and relate to one another, promote empathy, tune in to details we may be overlooking, and build perseverance and resilience.

They can propel us rather than what more people fear of keeping us stuck. A behind the therapy curtain piece of information is that I also show my students who are becoming counselors and psychologists this clip because we as clinicians need to be reminded that the goal is not for our clients to walk out of our office every day feeling happy; we would be shortchanging them and their potential for growth.

Lessons with the family

I'll share a memory of when our son was four years old and skinned his knee while playing in the front yard of a friend's house. I was sitting on the porch with my friend at the time who was the parent of four boys, two of which were close in age to our son. He comes running up the steps with tears and I pull him up onto my lap and give him a big hug. My friend went and got a bandage for his knee, and I can remember clear as day, she came and unaffectionately stuck it on rather than handing it to me. And her rather frosty response was to "stop crying, boys don't cry, go play." To say the least, I did not agree and was quite annoyed. I had a lot of things I wanted to say in that moment. Telling him to stop crying would just teach him to stuff things inside; it teaches him avoidance. I held him instead, embracing his tears, and we had our own conversation allowing him his emotion in that moment. And once he returned to play, she and I had a bit of a debate around the subject.

I know some of you reading this right now could be thinking that sounds just like your mom, dad, brother, etc. If it is your own words that you are hearing play back to you, then realize we start out as a product of our conditioning and what is modeled to us. I say "start out as" because we do not have to remain the same. With product testing (our experiences), focus groups (our friends and family) that provide feedback, AND some humility and willingness to embrace vulnerability, we undergo product improvement. You can start exploring your definition and meaning you make out of emotions to see how you may want to shift moving forward.

I know some children grow up being afraid to feel or express certain emotions as if the love towards them is conditional. I was very conscious with both of my children when they were incredibly young to let them know that I love them when they are happy, when they are sad, when they are scared, when they are mad, AND when I am happy, sad, angry, scared, mad. Because I know I am not a perfect parent, I knew there would be times I may not always respond the way I would have liked, so at minimum let me set them up with that foundation that my love is unconditional. I did not want them to worry that me being mad at something they did would mean that I did not love them in that moment. I know plenty of individuals who felt they had to earn their parents love growing up. I have an immense amount of gratitude for that sentiment of unconditional love being one of those things passed down to me from my own parents. And what is funny to me is that even though I frequently speak on this topic of the value of all our emotions to patients and students, in the moment with a sad kid, I may start getting like Joy and really appreciate the reminders and lessons from my own children.

My daughter at the age of seven looked a bit sad and quiet as we were getting ready for bed. I picture this moment with such pride as she tells me "Mommy, I will tell you why I am sad, but I don't want you to try to fix it." AW SNAP! Right?! She was telling me that it is important to let her have her sadness. I thought oh my goodness at just seven years old she realizes her emotions have purpose. How's that for emotional intelligence. It was the cutest thing to me and then as she told me she was sad because daddy was sick, and she was not supposed to get close to him so she could stay clear of his germs. She missed hugging him. I think she can have her sadness on that one. I have been amidst support groups and have heard many conversations around parents being fixers and it is so well-intentioned, yet we need to give ourselves permission to allow even our children to sit in their feelings and experience for the moment. This builds resilience, character, curiosity, and ingenuity.

We are a family that not only accepts but encourages emotional identification and expression. Admittedly I am the most animated and lively. I find it fortunate that my husband has no reservations about showing tears in front of our children. He scoffs at the stereotypes of what a man is and reveals courage and strength to be able to feel his vulnerability and then show it like a badge. I am proud that my children get this from him. Our son has also really taught me along the way as he is more of an introvert, and I can't assume things about his own emotions just because I may not see them displayed. I also know that we are not the only people that our children are exposed to, as many other messages get thrown at them daily. Our daughter clearly showed me an example of this at the age of six when she replied to a question of mine with, "Aren't you gonna ask me?" To which I replied, "ask you what?" and she finished with "if my inside voice matches my outside voice?" Look at that, already understanding how we may say one thing and feel another, how we may hold back our true thoughts and feelings on a matter.

SECTION 8

Trauma and Relationships

I t is not a far toss from emotions to navigating relationships as all that we covered thus far can make things a little topsy turvy when it comes to both friendships and intimate partners. People experiencing a trauma response often have difficulties in the areas of intimacy, trust, power and control, self-esteem, and safety. In our COVID-19 pandemic, many of us had our sense of power and control ripped out from under us, and it has affected the way we parent, the groceries we purchase, how we approach spending and financial planning, and our need to connect with friends and family. But those who are experiencing the pandemic as stress are typically capable of shifting to other thoughts, easily finding activities where they can forget their concerns and relax. They may display some worry and irritability, but to some degree they can maintain a feeling of control in their lives.

Many of the traumatic experiences that we hear from patients and clients occur in the context of interpersonal relationships. Van der Kolk (Ogden, 2006) explains that these traumas involve boundary violations, a loss of autonomous action, and a loss of self-regulation. These individuals "learn to respond to abuse and threats with mechanistic compliance or resigned submission"

(Ogden, 2006, p. 23 of foreward). These behaviors are reinforced and maintained into adult relationships often reported to clinicians in the form of caring for others' needs at the expense of their own. It makes absolute sense when viewing these with a trauma lens, yet to the individual themselves or to the partner in the relationship this can become a frustrating exchange. If your needs were not met in your earlier life experiences and you suffered abuse or neglect, of course you learned to neglect yourself and come to seek out relationships that almost mirror that as it is familiar to you. And in my experience, looking to build healthier responses and relationships is new and scary, and it can be much easier to stick with what is familiar (less scary even if unhealthy).

"I know this is a toxic relationship, but I almost go into a panic at the thought of not being with him." Heard this before? Why do good people find themselves stuck in toxic relationships? Therapists often speak of something called "love addiction," where a person craves the sense of fulfillment and validation that comes from being in a relationship, no matter how destructive. Although love addiction is not an official diagnosis, scientific literature highlights the intricate relationship between the need for love and validation, early childhood trauma, and substance use disorders.

Traumatic childhood experiences shape our perception of the world for the rest of our lives. Childhood trauma you learned is not limited to a violent trauma, like sexual abuse, physical abuse, or neglect, but could result from having parents who were not loving caregivers, or who failed to give validation at critical moments in a child's life. This can set up a near-pathological need to seek unconditional love and affection. At one level, this search for love stems from an inability to develop a healthy and internalized sense of self-worth in childhood. Severe and unwarranted criticism over the years is enough to throw off a person's ability to trust themselves, resulting in internalized messages of powerlessness, not being good enough or not being safe. As a result, any sense of value or worth in adulthood becomes defined solely by the relationship with other people. That internalization of criticism over time can make you more vulnerable to seeking a relationship where you must constantly prove your worth.

I also realize how vicious a cycle this really is, as some of you loved ones reading this may be that parent that did not provide the safe environment or the love and validation. And I imagine there is some work to be done in the relationship, or maybe it has already been done, in allowing some processing of the impact. There are many individuals who repeat the parenting that was delivered to them. We do not get a parenting class with a required passed exam like in applying for a driver's license. There may be some work towards forgiveness ahead of you and that may include both an amends to your loved one and forgiving yourself.

Often, people who experience complex trauma in their early familial relationships unconsciously try to recreate that dynamic. They might become involved in relationships that mimic the early negative experiences they had with an unavailable or potentially emotionally or physically abusive partner. It is as if the circumstances of the early experience are being recreated so they can have an opportunity to fix it and experience the unconditional love that was missing in the first relationship. This need going unmet can lead to an endless drive for closeness to the point that others may describe the person as needy, or the trauma survivor may use this label for themselves, which only further maintains shame. Healthy dynamics and give and take in relationships haven't been modeled though.

Some people approach relationship choices at a very conscious level, saying, "Oh, I need a partner who gets my adrenaline going, otherwise it gets boring." That has a lot to do with familiarity – people who grow up with chaos or emotional instability can develop the experience as their norm, which can impact what they seek in future relationships and leave them self-sabotaging potentially healthy relationships as it falls out of what they expect. Ironically, their unhealthy relationships create a feeling of safety.

It is not uncommon to have conversations with those in these situations who speak about how although potentially unsafe, in reality, a toxic relationship becomes familiar. And remember what I already said about something that is familiar is less scary than something that is safe but unknown or not experienced before.

The "high" from what is referred to as "love addiction" is remarkably like what we see in gambling addiction, which is built around variable reinforcement. The relationship, which once started in a honeymoon-like state, devolves to mostly negative interactions. Then, BAM! there is one pleasant experience that seems to make up for all the destructive ones. It's like making a lucky pull on a slot machine, a big rush that makes you forget that when you add everything up, you're losing money. That is one of the strongest types of reinforcements, and it contributes to keeping people in unhealthy relationships, chasing the rush they get from intermittent and unpredictable (variable ratio) positive reinforcement.

Let me add that for any of you that happen to be the partner of someone with a trauma history, that you may be thinking wait a minute, it isn't me- its them. Maybe you are frustrated and confused when your partner resists every compliment you try to deliver. Think about how compliments may have been used as a manipulation tactic by an abuser. Now, those kind words have lost their value as they believe there is a hidden agenda or motives.

You may find that you often feel as if your partner is stirring up drama or making issues out of things that don't really exist. Or they are just not sharing your perspective on things. Fears of abandonment may be what is behind them picking a fight that allows them to be in control of leaving instead of getting left. And you may be thinking what the heck because you were not even thinking about leaving just because you were in a disagreement. But your partner's radar for danger and threats to themselves needs some mechanic work. And now that you are getting a basic understanding of the impact of trauma you can also respond in a healthier way.

Your relationship may not fit into the label of toxic and it can still have aspects of it that are unhealthy and tear at the fabric of your bond. Maybe your partner holds unrelenting standards, or rigid rules and expectations of how the relationship *should* be. It could be that this hypercritical mindset is held towards you, or maybe it is held internally towards their own behaviors, actions, appearance, etc. They also may have these standards they wished they could have held a caregiver to, and now project them onto you. This person may feel like they must be in total control so that something bad does not happen.

The person may have developed a sense that their safety in relationships comes by making sure others are happy. Another pattern is someone becoming overly submissive to another person's wants or requests for fear that if they express a different interest or opinion, that they will lose them. They may go into a panic after an argument and engage in behaviors to try to pull the partner back in. This person may not be working from a strong place of object constancy.

Your partner may hold you at a distance which serves purpose- "If I don't let people in, I don't get hurt." What they spend less time considering is- at what cost? Social isolation is another behavior we see where the person alienates themselves from the very needed support network as they believe they are inferior and if they truly let people in to know them, they will not be cared for, or it will not turn out as hoped. It could be biting sarcasm, push-pull behaviors, ultimatums, silent treatment, not communicating needs and wants, tit-for-tat behaviors, and you can fill in your own blank here, I'm sure. After all, whose marriage is perfect?

It is my belief that our society in general, without the addition of trauma, has a bit of a skewed expectation of what a healthy relationship or marriage is. I have heard countless individuals say that marriage should not require this much work, or we should not be having this many disagreements. Says who!? If it did not entail that side of it then why do the traditional vows call for in sickness/health, rich/poor, and in good times AND bad?

One of my favorite films I showed my children is Disney's *Into the Woods* (originally a Broadway musical) because of twists and turns that are not so typical of many of the fairytales told. Happily Ever After does not have to (and although I try to watch my should statements, should not) mean devoid of challenges and obstacles. I think for a lot of young girls especially, there has been a common thread for years of implied messages that you have to be rescued and taken care of and everything will be dreamy. Many of the fairytales show obstacles and challenges leading up to falling in love and then love makes it all better. Whereas, *Into the Woods* shows that those things come even after, and that love is not a linear path we travel.

What is shown on television and the theaters influences the belief systems that people enter a marriage with, just as much as what they see at home. Gender role expectations are often the first of these challenges when relationships are starting out and what you believe the other person *should* be doing in the relationship. You each come in with a belief about what your roles need to be, and they may not necessarily be right or wrong. Together you need to explore what is *right* for this relationship and it becomes a negotiation hopefully on both ends and can be one that is ever shifting over the years.

The challenges and obstacles you face can make a partnership stronger and even grow commitment to each other, barring you make the effort to continue improving your communication and delivery. I can think of times when I have even said something to my husband like "you know what I meant" or "you should've known" and when I think with a rational mind- How? I cannot expect my thoughts and emotions to be broadcasted outside of my own head, nor to expect everyone else's to be what mine are, just as he cannot expect that; what an egocentric and child-like (remember that developmentally) place to live in. This tears down relationships and I don't care how many years you have been together; you are not mind readers.

Now imagine all of that coupled with the impact of past trauma on one's behaviors, belief systems, expectations, boundaries, and so on.

Our boundaries impact our choices.

Our boundaries with others directly impact how are we treated by others in our relationships. People who suffer from love addiction often never developed a healthy set of boundaries between themselves and others in close, personal relationships. This is especially true if parents or guardians did not model healthy boundaries, were always fighting or triangulated their child into the role of mediator, affecting the grown child's ability to know what should be expected from a healthy relationship.

There are two types of unhealthy boundaries that we often explore in treatment. One type of boundary holds others at a distance, because it helps them feel protected and safe and minimizes the potential for conflict. The cost of this sort of boundary is people do not feel connected in their relationships. They are lonely and lack the support that could come from a warmer, more emotionally intimate relationship. Simply put, if you are always pushing people away emotionally, it is really challenging to have an intimate relationship. The other person might feel neglected, or they might sense that you are keeping yourself closed off. When the relationship breaks up, it serves as a reinforcement for all those negative messages that have been internalized: "I'm not lovable" or "I have to do what it takes to find love."

The second type of unhealthy boundary is a fused, or what some in the field (although there is not total agreement on the use of the word) may term codependent boundary, where a person is porous like a sponge and soaks up their partner's identity. People who have fused themselves with their partner are more likely to accept poor treatment in a relationship, and fearful of what would happen if they don't. It might seem like they value their romantic partner above themselves. While they can feel connected, they neglect to care for themselves. They may not even know what they value or prioritize because they have become so enmeshed with the other person.

It is not uncommon for people to bounce from one boundary style to another. In one relationship, they might hold themselves apart, protecting themselves. Their next relationship might have them moving to the other extreme, becoming completely absorbed by their partner's identity. In counseling, we try to help people recognize the pattern of their choices. While remaining distant in a relationship might once have served an adaptive purpose, this response comes at a cost. Likewise, a person enmeshed in a relationship may not realize he/she is experiencing abuse because they are just so grateful that their partner "loves" them. Often, though, it is not until there is a significant personal toll that people become motivated to look at their relationship patterns.

Every relationship seeks its own equilibrium, and what works for one couple might seem strange for another. But how can you tell if your relationship is truly unhealthy for you? What can you do? Awareness is the first step. We cannot change something if we do not know it is there. Obviously, nothing is perfect, and any relationship is going to have its difficulties. However, it is important that people can be their authentic selves in a relationship and that we strive for communication that is respectful. And when it is not, partners learn humility and make changes. If you evaluate your relationship and find that the difficulties outweigh the positives, I encourage you to take steps to probe this further.

You can start by looking at how your past experiences have shaped your current relationship. You may have developed a set of conditioned, automatic responses that interfere with your ability to develop an authentic relationship. I think about an experiential exercise I have seen used several times in a group or marital therapy session where you put bricks in a backpack to represent certain things experienced and taken away from previous relationships. Then put that backpack on and see how much your past experiences are weighing you down in your present one, or even in your life as a single person.

This reminds me of a story I have shared for years ever since I first saw it mentioned on the internet. It floats around on multiple sites and is replicated with different images and video clips, and I have seen it for several years yet still haven't found the originator. The story is of a psychology professor that walked around on a stage while teaching stress management principles to an auditorium filled with students. She holds up a glass of water and although most are waiting for her to ask if they see it as half full or half empty, she asks them how heavy it is. Students start shouting out answers ranging from a few ounces to a couple pounds. She then replies that the weight of the glass itself does not matter, from her perspective, what is more important in answering its heaviness is how long she holds it. If she holds it for a minute or two it is light and in no way inconvenient. If she holds it into an hour her arm is starting to ache, and longer still, her arm may cramp and become numb to the point of it feeling paralyzed which results in dropping the glass to the floor. The longer we carry around the pain of our past, the heavier it feels and the more likely it is to get in our way of functioning. This goes back to that avoidance because it is keeping everything in the backpack still. Avoidance is NOT going to empty it.

With all that said, let us not confuse obstacles, challenges, and difficulties with abuse in a relationship. Some signs of an unhealthy relationship that could have potential for abuse include walking on eggshells around your partner for fear that they will get angry, not respecting boundaries, minimizing your accomplishments or belittling you directly or to others, becoming increasingly isolated from family and friends, and feeling controlled by another person. We also live in a culture that at times accepts and romanticizes unhealthy or abusive behavior like pushing, shoving, or slapping.

We must be clear that abuse is not love. This may be challenging to wrap one's head around if they have experienced trauma in their past. Those who experienced abuse (verbal, emotional, physical, sexual, and even financial) earlier on in childhood are especially vulnerable to unhealthy relationships later in life because of internalized messages, what becomes familiar to them, and in some cases- the source of safety also being the source of threat. Some individuals become unable to distinguish safety within a relationship and again, what may be new and healthy may also feel scary and unfamiliar.

There is a lot of pressure placed on these individuals with questions of why they stay in the relationship. We are so often putting the focus on the survivor's behavior and what they did or didn't do, or what they should have known, and even the comments that make me cringe of how they may have allowed it to happen. Even those who knew and saw the signs, and who wanted to leave, the question then became "what do I do now?" as the challenges may seem insurmountable with considerations of housing, childcare, transportation, legal assistance, and finances. Rather, it behooves us to look at how our society and culture support and condone the behaviors of the perpetrators and how our inaction in that regard further permits it.

We question how the survivor missed the signs, but in my experience with patients, they did not miss them at all, they just did not know what to do once they saw them. When we start placing blame on the person being abused for not leaving, or the family for not catching signs, what we do is take the blame off where it is rightfully owed- on the perpetrator. We also need to get better as a society in what we allow both indirectly and directly in terms of condoning and excusing inappropriate behavior of those displaying it on all levels.

For loved ones who are well-intended and wanting so badly to tell the survivors to leave the relationship it is important to understand there needs to be some planning around this instead of just urging. The most dangerous period in abusive relationships is when the person being abused leaves. This leaves the perpetrator with nothing to lose, and we have seen it result in countless cases of tragedy. Therefore, it is so important that family members and friends do not rush to pressure their loved one to leave without getting the appropriate assistance and resources in place. If you have a friend or loved one you suspect may be in an unsafe relationship, the best action you can take is to make sure they know you support them unconditionally. Offer to be a resource i.e., if they need a ride to a center or a therapist, or to watch the kids so they can take steps to safely extricate themselves.

A person in an unhealthy relationship may already feel substantial guilt and shame so it is important not to blame or judge them. Instead, let them know they are not alone and make it clear you are available for them. Isolation is a tactic an abusive person will use to continue to control them. If there is a survivor reading this and feeling encouraged to look at options, therapists and centers trained in trauma and domestic violence exist and often offer free resources to help you understand your situation and support a safe and confidential exit strategy if appropriate.

Watch What You Say

G oing to therapy can leave one feeling vulnerable and uncertain and a therapist may explore and have conversation around what you may feel like after leaving a session, having just opened up about something so personal. Some clinicians may approach the shame and guilt in session and the fears that may exist in the client of how the therapist views them. I may ask what they need to know right now about my beliefs about them, so they don't reinforce these beliefs with their own internal dialogue.

We must be careful though in how we probe individuals for their histories. I think many well-intended people (clinicians/ other professionals and family/friends) too often try to jump in too quick and want to explore the details of the events but that itself can contribute to a re-traumatization or becoming emotionally dysregulated, which pushes them further away from seeking the help they need. That piece of it can be left to trauma informed and trained clinicians. On the other end, we see again both clinicians and family/friends shy away from having conversations around trauma when someone is being vulnerable and sharing because of personal discomfort or fear that talking about it will make them feel bad. That kind of avoidance can increase the shame that the individual feels already.

I have also had patients express to me that they felt their family members directly or indirectly expressed that their trauma is something not to be discussed because it was too painful on the other person (like a child telling their parent that she was abused was too painful for them to hear and carry because it may be received as a message that they weren't a good parent). Or having a felt experience of having to be quiet so that it could go away, so that we can forget that it happened. Additionally, there may be fear that they will not be believed by their loved ones, which had been a realistic concern for many of my past patients.

Another thing I would want adults to be cautioned about is a line of questioning that implies blame on the survivor- what did you do, why did you go there, how could you have, what were you thinking...? As that just serves to instill the belief that it was their fault- and to be frank, no matter what decisions we may make before someone harms us- it never gives that person permission to do it. For ex. "Being in the wrong place" or having poor judgment about a person still does not give that person consent.

We know that a protective factor is having a strong relationship with someone where the trauma can be disclosed and be received without a response that either indirectly implies or is explicitly stated that projects blame onto the individual. When you know someone is in a domestic violence situation and you see a bruise on their face, the last thing you want to do is ask them "What did you do?" We have seen the likes of this in legal proceedings which still have a reciprocal relationship with the stigma of abuse in society and how a survivor of a sexual assault can be on the stand having their entire dating history or wardrobe on display. We face this struggle especially when substances are involved where a person went out for drinks with a person and then is assaulted. Saying yes to drinking is not the same as saying yes to sex. And one can say yes, and then change their mind and that becomes the answer- No.

And when we put the blame on the person who was assaulted, who do we take the blame off? That goes for any situation, when we take the blame on ourselves for a buddy dying in combat, we take the blame off the person who shot them. It is one thing to wish that something didn't happen, it is another thing to take on the responsibility for it. I have heard some respected men, who I will not name, make comments of how a man's behavior towards a woman is excused and given a pass if that woman dressed a certain way. What a horrible thing to teach, that I as a woman can control a man's behavior with my clothes, but not with my words when I say no.

It is also especially important not to minimize someone's experience with phrases like "it could have been worse" or "just get over it." That can be very invalidating and will prevent the individual from disclosing further. Making meaning is important across our lives. Remember what was stated earlier about us being little scientists from the moment we step into the world. We work to organize information and to make sense of it. My caution around watching what you say and the language you use is both an advisory for loved ones on how they may speak to the person who survived trauma, AND for the trauma survivor to guard what they internally digest of their own self-talk. Some of the most important conversations we will ever have will be those with ourselves. We use filters for air conditioners to block out the toxins and pollutants from entering the system. Where is you filter? What words do you digest (of others and your own)?

You may have been taught, indirectly and directly, the just world belief that is tied to the image of a manageable and predictable world. Have you ever thought that good things happen to good people and bad things happen to bad people? As children we learn that our good behavior is rewarded and that we have punishments or consequences for our bad behavior. Or that people get what they deserve? Can you imagine what this does to the minds of those who have experienced trauma?

Walker (2020) notes that we like to be in control and when we are not, particularly in times of crisis, it can be disruptive, and we are left trying to find where we do have control. Sometimes taking on responsibility for what happened, although assigned to the wrong person, still serves purpose in making sense out of an experience in finding a way to have been in control of it. Because the counter argument of not being the one who is responsible for the trauma leaves a lot of fear and vulnerability in the realization that we can't control everything.

Growing up with a belief that the world is fair and then experiencing something traumatic often leaves one reading into the story that they must have done something bad to deserve it, after all the world is fair so I must have done something wrong. Or I can look to find what I could have done to prevent it because I am in control of my life. But, maybe for you or your loved one, the messages received early on were of being a bad kid and not having control over anything, which leaves this individual saying "see, I deserved it" or "it proves I have no control." We engage in assimilation, which often means that new information is distorted or changed, again so that we can make sense of it (Broderick & Blewitt, 2020). I can recall a patient once talking about coming to terms with powerlessness over what happened to her and how freeing it finally was. She shared that although it may feel safer to assign the control over to oneself, the well-intended purpose left so much shame for something that really wasn't her fault.

"Emotional memory can also convert the past into an expectation of the future and can make the worst experiences of our past persist as felt realities" (Ecker et. al., 2012, p.6). It can lead people to making an over-accommodation which is future oriented thinking that generalizes others, the self, and the world. It can lead to a belief that the world is generally a dangerous place. Or that others can't be trusted, and you can't get close to anyone. Before the truth can set you free, you need to recognize which lie is holding you hostage (Rachel Wolchin). Maybe the lie is something you are telling yourself about your worth, who you are, or your purpose.

Back to social psychology, we engage in confirmation bias that impacts not only how we gather information, but also how we recall information or how we make meaning or interpretation out of it. This means we pay attention to information that supports our prior belief. If we believe people can't be trusted, then naturally we start to find all the evidence of how we were wronged and taken advantage of. We may be filtering out individuals in our lives or situations where trust was intact.

A classic example that I use with both individuals I have treated and in the classroom with students may help illustrate. I start by telling them to look around the room and say to themselves (not out loud) all the things in the room with the color _____. I left it blank because you need to take stock of the room first before you pick the color. I just did this the other day in class and used the color black. I tell them as they are looking around the room to pay close attention and find everything with the color black and say it in their heads. Then I have them close their eyes or look at the floor if that is more comfortable, and then I tell them to continue repeating the things that are black in their heads to try to remember them well (Like how we can ruminate over those negative thoughts about ourselves, others, and the world). I then ask them to say out loud all the things in the room with the color red. There's silence! Then some giggles.

Finally, I have them open their eyes and tell me why that was difficult. Many of them respond to me "well you said look for black" as if I made a mistake by then asking for red. I explain to them that it was on purpose to show how easily we can miss things, pieces of information, and you can see how this impacts recall. And what cracked me up this time is that I have several students in this class (on brief counseling) that had me in the previous semester for an addiction course, where I did the same exercise, and they were duped again. They laughed about it too.

One day I did this in a psychoeducational group with patients and was wearing red pants and glasses. Initially I thought I should've picked another color because they will get this one for sure because it is too obvious. They still didn't have an answer when I later asked for the red items. One day I had a tiny red sticky note on my papers that most of them couldn't see from where they were sitting. I pointed it out to show that just because they cannot see it, does not mean it doesn't exist. This helps to highlight how the lenses we are looking through shapes what we are taking in and we need to adjust the lenses.

How does this relate to trauma? It has everything to do with the issue of self-blame. Your loved one may have spent years looking for or focusing on 'evidence' that supports inaccurate beliefs about what happened. In hindsight, it is easy to say that you should have known. What we see a lot of in the field is people recalling verbally only pieces of the puzzle and leaving out details that support the trauma not being their fault. Although we have learned how trauma is stored and how much is a body and symptom experience, the meaning we make out of what happens to us has powerful consequences. A colleague of mine who I have run trauma psychoeducational groups with once commented in a group that people don't do well with ties in sporting events, we need an answer. We need to be in control of at least that, making sense of something.

I use a potentially benign scenario of receiving a wedding invitation to illustrate the connection between our thoughts and our actions or behaviors and how important the thoughts can really be. Picture it (O dear, for those who know me I am sure there was a chuckle as you know I am a fanatic for Golden Girls and now I have to leave it in), you receive a wedding invitation and maybe your reaction is thinking things like "this sucks, now I have to spend money on a nice outfit," or "I am going to have to be social," or possibly "the talk is all going to be superficial and I have to put on a fake smile." What are the emotions that come up as you read those lines- annoyance, dread? Are there behaviors that follow, like isolating or looking for a drink? Yet, someone else may receive that invitation and think "yay I have something to get dressed up for, how nice since we haven't been social since before the pandemic," or "I will get to see my cousin that always makes me laugh." This person feels excited.

We too often assert cause and effect with things that happen and what follows. What this shows us is that we may be missing something. If the wedding invitation caused the first person to feel dread, then the second person should feel the same. The reason the same wedding invitation elicits two different responses is because of the thoughts that ensue, the meaning we make, the interpretation. When something bad happens to you and you begin to think you are damaged goods, will never find happiness, and will never be good enough, those are thoughts holding you hostage.

And to connect it back to self-blame again I will use a frequent example that has come up working with women who have experienced sexual assault. The line I often hear refers to them being at fault because of a revealing outfit they wore. If we try to put some rational thought to it, if wearing that short dress for example was the reason they were assaulted, then every other time they wore that dress it should have happened, right? If it was their fault because of being at the bar that night, then the 50 other times they went to that same bar would mean that they should have been assaulted then too. And then we could infer that anyone else wearing a short dress there that night would have been assaulted too. Sometimes we just need to put things that way for the survivor themselves, and potentially for any of you loved ones that entertained any of this faulty thinking.

I have heard others' thoughts around future relationships, like "If I get close to people, I'll get hurt." And the response they have next is "I'd rather be alone than hurt," which is only comparing two negative possibilities. The thought of being able to trust even one person hasn't popped into their minds. And we start making those thoughts and beliefs out to be the likely scenario, rather than more realistically seeing it as possible. There is a significant difference between something being possible vs likely. As Dorothy once told Rose in Golden Girls when afraid to take a chance in a relationship, "If you take a chance sometimes good things happen and sometimes bad things happen. But if you don't take a chance, nothing happens."

I encourage people to look at what they've been telling themselves for so long, to look at the evidence they've been building and see if it is really fact-based or just habit thinking. We know how much impact trauma has on the body, how emotional memories and symptoms show up, that traditional talk therapy is often not enough, and we still cannot forget that the way a person makes meaning out of the event is also important in the healing process. A person's perception of the event, not the event itself can keep people stuck.

Especially when I am having conversations with clients who are now connecting to the material on how trauma impacts the brain, they speak about how they talk to themselves after displaying some of that behavior covered earlier. They had said negative things about who they are as a person and only see themselves as that being the whole pie of who they are rather than just one piece of it. Hulk is a part of Bruce Banner, and Bruce is so many other things like intelligent and kind. We need to curb the all-or nothing thinking and watch the conversation we are having with ourselves.

You may open a bag of grapes and pull one out that is the nastiest and most rotten you have ever tasted. But if I were to guess, you dig for other grapes or look around in the bag as you could still have a good bag overall and just need to throw out a few spoiled ones. But when we have a bad grape that is a real-life person doing harm to us, our body and mind work to protect us from all the other bad grapes out there. Unfortunately, this leaves you with missed opportunities to experience good things in your life, whether it be new experiences, close relationships with others, or being able to feel comfortable within yourself.

SECTION 10

Some Things You Can Do

I t is not my belief that someone must suffer from trauma for a lifetime. I have seen healing in patients that is remarkable, whereby the end of treatment they no longer meet criteria for a diagnosis of PTSD. Trauma survivors have strength beyond belief. Anyone sitting across from the clinician has resources or they wouldn't be sitting in front of them right now. It is important to frame it this way for patients and to ask them to think about things like "What got you through that?" because they may not know their own resources. We see progress begin when these individuals start to shift the way they look at their responses. Once seeing them as pathological and now viewing them as solutions they came up with to a problem. I see a lot of self-compassion develop when this happens. We need more of that, especially when you read about how much the language and internal dialogue play a role. The good news is there is help and people can become informed and empowered to change behavior patterns and have healthy and happy relationships moving forward. Therapists cannot change the past for anyone, but we can help clients change their relationship with their past to develop healthier and more adaptive responses and partnerships.

If you're concerned about relationship choices, I recommend undertaking this exploration with therapeutic support. A trauma-informed counselor can help you unravel the past in a safe way and figure out how it affects your current relationship dynamics. If you attempt to do this on your own, you may get caught up in negative internal self-talk that doesn't support your growth and could even drive substance use. With the same caution, couples counseling may not be the right choice for you depending on the dynamics of the relationship. If there is current abuse, it may serve you better to seek out a clinician to have initial conversations about the issues and decide how to safely proceed from there.

Grounding techniques/coping skills

Some of you may have heard of the term grounding technique before. This is when you tune in to sensory experiences to allow you to step away from some unwanted recall, flashback, dissociation, or negative thoughts by becoming present focused. This is not treatment and doesn't resolve their symptoms, yet it acts like a pause button to allow that frontal lobe to come back online and allow you to function with rational thought.

If you are with someone who could benefit from some grounding, you can ask them to name some things for you- the date, time, items in the room. You can also have them perform a quick task like naming everything in the room that is square, or things that are yellow. There are tasks involving the five senses like naming 5 things that you see, 4 that you can touch, 3 that you hear, 2 that you smell, and 1 that you taste. One thing I tell my clients is that it is ok if you mix that up, the point is simply to get focused on your surroundings so if you can't name that many items its fine. They could engage in a distraction task of giving you their to-do list or listing their favorite sports teams. I also have asked people to wiggle their toes or describe the texture of their arm rest.

There are a variety of skills, tasks, exercises, and activities that people engage in as a coping mechanism when presented with stress, intense emotions, unhelpful thoughts, and the like. Coping skills don't have to be monumental or sophisticated. They can be simple and yet I recognize that simple doesn't always mean easy to implement. Simple and easy are two different things. The list is endless and can include going for a walk, stretching, doodling, finding ways to LAUGH (watch your favorite comedian), reciting a favorite scripture, connecting with nature, identifying gratitude, and so on.

When trauma related reactions are occurring, healthy coping skills can be used to manage them more effectively as well as to alter the neural pathways that have been leading to such reactions. Coping skills that can be helpful to manage triggers fall into multiple categories and can include connection with others, mindfulness, sensory activities, movement/physical, and breathing techniques. A past supervisor of mine packed jars for blowing bubbles and Play-doh for our groups on coping skills. That sensory experience with the texture can be relaxing for some (think about stress balls and other sand or clay items out in the marketplace). And blowing bubbles? Yes, think about it through a lens of a breathing exercise. Family members can help in the healing process by displaying patience and understanding, compassion, helping them to establish a sense of safety, and modeling and encouraging the use of healthy coping skills.

Here is the important piece though about coping skills to make them effective, you've got to engage in them when you don't need them. The analogy I often use with clients is that of a fire drill. The purpose of a drill is for you to know where your exits are and what to do when you are in a crisis. If you wait until you're in need of your coping skills to then pull them out, you're likely going to resort to your old response patterns. You need to utilize them when you are having a good day as well; the more familiar you become with your exits, the stronger the chance you will use them first.

Believe in change

Some of the individuals I have worked with in treatment have been so beaten down by themselves, others, their symptoms, and their experiences that they have lost hope for the future that it can be anything different or anything better. I can remember so many conversations that would come up after learning how trauma impacts the brain and some responding "now what!" Many almost became even more discouraged initially in recognizing what their experiences have done to their brain and body. With further exploration and conversation, they begin to grow that self-compassion in understanding primarily that they aren't all those negative adjectives that they, and others, once used for them because of their behavior. We help them begin to find their window of tolerance, regain a sense of safety, try new ways of assessing situations and responding in kind.

I began using an exercise to help channel all that education into hopefulness and have found it to be a standout both in groups and individually. In total it takes about two minutes and involves folding paper. If you would like to do it with me now, then you will need to get a blank piece of paper (a typical writing tablet or printer size). Hold it vertically/portrait position and fold it in half bringing the top down to meet the bottom. Crease it well. As you make your crease, you may even think about a behavior or a reaction that has been around for a long time that you often regret or would like to be different. Now fold your paper in half again bringing your right side to the left and making a firm crease again. You will keep folding your paper in half until you really can't anymore and with each crease you think about that behavior, or even multiple ones.

Now, open your paper all the way. Next, fold your paper in all the same ways as you just did, the same pattern until it is at its smallest. Open it back up, and then fold it all again one more time. Trust me there is a point to this. Open it up now and think for a moment what this may represent…Don't peak at the next sentence. What I often get from the individuals and groups is "Habit behavior" or some wording along those lines. Think how fast and easy it gets to fold it back down the smallest size once those creases are made. How easy it is to respond in the same unhealthy way that you have been.

We need part 2 to bring home the message. Now with your paper open and unfolded, I want you to make a brand-new fold in half, instead of bringing the top to the bottom, bring the right to the left. When you crease it, think about a coping skill or another tool that you've learned that you could insert. And keep making new folds until your smallest size. Open it up and think what this can represent. Our new folds are like creating new behaviors and responses. It shows us that it is possible. Inevitably, I have someone voice something like "yea but it's messy." Yep, it sure is, and that is also what treatment may feel like at times. And it can be messy and still possible.

Another example is taking a short cut through a bunch of grass. If you walk over that enough times you will flatten it down and it will start to look like a distinct path. If you start walking parallel to it yet ten feet over, that grass path will grow in and a new one will form. The imagery of the grass and the folding paper exercise helps illustrate neuroplasticity, which is your brain's ability to rewire itself, where neural pathways make new connections. It is a growth process and is fostered by inhibition of old responses coupled with repetition of new and more adaptive responses (out with the old, in with the new).

We also encourage them to have patience with themselves and would encourage you all as their family members to be mindful of this as a process as well. Even for students and clinicians new to trauma informed care can benefit from that reminder, that change doesn't happen overnight. Although trauma impacts the brain, it is so important to realize that healing does too! The therapeutic journey and growth will also bring with it brain changes.

Reinforce change

What is the hope when you give a child a lollipop for being polite? That they will be polite again. Our behavior gets shaped by what follows it. And changing behavior that has existed for a long time is possible, may take time, and needs reinforcement. Understanding operant conditioning can help with behavior change. Skinner (1938) introduced us to a type of learning in which behaviors are influenced by the consequences that follow them. Operant conditioning is an associative learning as we associate our own actions with consequences. He posed that we behave in predictable ways because of the rewards we experience or because of the need to avoid or escape aversive consequences.

A reinforcer is defined by the function it serves and what is reinforcing to one, isn't always reinforcing to another. One of the mistakes made in everyday language is looking at the terms positive and negative reinforcement as something that is good vs bad, respectively. What I teach my clients and students is to look at the words like math symbols: positive will be a + (addition) and negative will be a − (minus or subtraction). Positive reinforcers are those that bring some pleasure and have the result of strengthening behavior. Some examples include praise, attention, money, and food. Negative reinforcers are those that take away something aversive or unpleasurable. Putting on your seatbelt makes the nagging alert stop (take the sound away). A teenager has chores removed from their list because of good grades.

You may reinforce some things intentionally, whereas others happen unintentionally. If you tell a funny story in a group and everyone laughs, you are more likely to tell that story again. Someone with an eating disorder or intense focus on their appearance and weight may get reinforcement when someone who hasn't seen them in a while says, "you look great." If a child is screaming at a restaurant for a treat and stops when you give in, you will be negatively reinforced by taking away the embarrassing screams and facial expressions from onlookers and will be more inclined to hand them a treat the next time. The child is also reinforced, but positively as they received something pleasurable, so the next time they know they just need to embarrass you enough and you will cave. Remember I mentioned the attention that is received from a child hitting their sibling? We may see it as negative, but it is still attention nonetheless, so they are actually being positively reinforced.

When we try to change a behavior, we can expect some challenges. For the example with the child and the treat, if we stop giving in, we may see an increase in their attempt because they don't understand why it isn't working. They may even up the ante. You've got to ride it out and then at some point they learn that the behavior doesn't get them the treat anymore and they stop doing it. Being prepared for these rebounds helps our expectations and potential follow through.

You may see this in family systems for example. I think about a film that is shown in the substance use arena a lot where the wife goes away to a residential treatment facility. At home, the husband had a role for a long time of a family manager, he rescued and cleaned up situations so that his wife wouldn't face the consequences, especially with their daughters. He was reinforced in this role too by praise, thanks, and feeling needed. His behaviors had purpose. When she returned home and was maintaining her sobriety, he felt left out and struggled to figure out that his role would need to change and then what it would even look like.

This can happen when anyone in a relationship makes a change, it throws off the status quo. If we want to change a behavior/role, we need to be conscious of reinforcing the new one to maintain progress. In a previous work setting, we had a 'catch them being good' initiative in the vein of reinforcing the behaviors that we wanted to see. When a client makes a change in treatment, we/they need to explore what is a reinforcer for them, and then how to start utilizing it to continue the progress. If your old behavior got a lot more attention, watch out for it trying to show its face again, simply because the new one isn't getting reinforced to stick around. The steps you are making towards change, no matter how small you deem them, awareness, implementing a new behavior, a new outlook or thought process, be sure to recognize it.

Gratitude

There is an experience of posttraumatic growth that is less referenced than PTSD, and learning that negative experiences can spur positive change, including a recognition of personal strength, the exploration of new possibilities, improved relationships, a greater appreciation for life, and spiritual growth" (Tedeschi, 2020). Tedeschi and Calhoun (1996) also developed scales that look for responses in a variety of areas including spiritual growth and they are revising it to look at existential themes that may connect more with those who don't ascribe to a religion (Tedeschi & Calhoun, 1996).

This growth has to do with maintaining a sense of hope about surviving through trauma and not having to be passive victims, and that the person can have positive personality and life changes happen as a result. To help facilitate this growth, one needs to learn how to acknowledge and embrace pain rather than reject it, which is common in mindfulness practice. Notice, that does not mean being okay with it as many people misperceive when they hear a mindfulness concept like *acceptance*. We cannot move forward from something that we do not accept as existing in the first place. Struggling with reality is wasted struggle. When we wrestle with accepting what has happened, we keep it in our present, rather than moving it to our past that we can grow beyond. It is about finding a way to channel your pain to work for your benefit. Yet, we do have to own what has been lost in the process to be able to then find a way to live with that. And this must be done with caution and not diving right in to explore it so that we don't minimize the pain they have endured.

Gratitude has been backed by research for several benefits on physical and mental health and many are finding it useful to engage in daily gratitude reflections (mostly morning or at bedtime or simply when in hopeless and unhelpful thinking). These don't have to be monumental things you are thankful for, and it doesn't mean you are dismissing the gravity of the situation or the loss you or many others are experiencing. I know that virtual schooling during the pandemic brought on other consequences to juggle. One parent shared with me that having her children home pushed her to find gratitude in the whole family getting to wake up a little later in the home as they didn't have to factor in the prep time of packing lunches and the kids having enough time to get ready and hop on a bus or in a car. That extra hour or 90 minutes of sleep also had ripple effects of less dragging of the kids and better moods, so she noticed they were all getting along better.

In treatment, I tell patients that an example is having gratitude directed at themselves for showing up to programming. That may have been the last thing they felt like doing due to withdrawal symptoms, amotivation, ambivalence, etc. yet they still showed up. At times I will encourage a nightly routine of finding an internal piece to be thankful for- I was encouraging to a friend today, I was loyal, or I was honest. And then find an external piece- being thankful for a partner, therapist, or a clean house with working water. Your brain can go all kinds of places with this.

Self-care

In wanting to care for your loved ones, don't forget about caring for yourself. We're instructed on a plane to put our oxygen mask on first before those we are caring for. Bring on the awareness, balance, and connection. Helpers need to take time to self-reflect. We must also find ways to take care of our physical bodies whether that be by fueling our body with nutritious healthy foods or maintaining an exercise routine, we must find a way to care for our bodies. We can't be good or useful to others if we are driving on empty.

SECTION 11

In Closing

My years in this field have shown me the astounding innate drive and ability to heal; trauma doesn't have to define us. However, it's critical to invest the time to understand how our past experiences affect our self-love and intimate relationships with others so that we can build a toolbox to cope in a healthy way and develop fulfilling relationships.

There's a quote with no real solid agreement as to who said it (a variety of famous figures), that suggests everyone you meet is fighting a battle that you may know nothing about and for that, you should remain kind. And don't forget to turn that kindness inward for battles you've faced and won. I will leave you with something a family member shared (gave me permission to include it) "I forgive myself, for not knowing what I do know now. I love myself and I love that child that was hurting all those years. She is free now; she is at peace."

Where I work, I see every individual that comes through our doors as having innate healing and growth potential that just needs to be tapped into in conjunction with appropriate education, awareness, and treatment. Don't be discouraged by setbacks as there isn't always a linear path to where you are aiming to be, and no two people will carve out the exact same path. What works for one doesn't necessarily work for the next one so stop comparing yourself to others. When you turn off course while driving with navigation, it simply re-routes you, right? The twists and turns along the way don't have to keep you from your destination. Trauma is not something we choose, but Healing is.

Acknowledgements

F irst and foremost, I give a heartfelt and public display of gratitude to my family. Jeremiah, thank you for always believing in me and helping me see this project through. I am sure you lost count at how many times you heard me say "just one more thing." You and I have been through some challenges in our lives and are true stories of resilience. We have persevered through trauma and obstacles that can rock a marriage to its core. I am proud of the man you are. I am honored to be by your side, now almost half my life, pulling through and staying committed to the bigger picture. I am thankful for us holding our love as our foundation to be more than the bad days that are now behind us and those that will be before us and more than anyone or anything that tries to get between us (catch that reference? SHMILY). I am proud of us.

Angelo and Ava- you have given me joy and inspiration more than you will ever know. I thank you and daddy for your patience and acceptance as I devoted my time to my work and this book. On the hardest of days when all I wanted was to be home, you found your ways to let me know I was missed, yet still appreciated me managing my roles. I am thankful for all that you teach me. Angelo, I am loving the stimulating conversations we engage in and watching you mature into a kind, responsible, and thoughtful young man. Ava, your affection is infectious; thank you for all the extra snuggles. You inspire me in ways you will never know. ("Always find a way, 'cause that's what winners do"- Big Z).

To my parents, Joe, and Goia- I am grateful for you being everything I needed. The lessons you've taught my brother (love you bro) and me have shaped my life in ways you may not expect. In my days as a nationally competitive gymnast, I remember wanting to quit after a really bad fall. You didn't let me because it was out of fear. My ability to pull through at so many different points in my life was birthed in experiences like that. My passion for the work around equity and inclusion was planted in the modeling you gave in appreciating the dignity of others. Thank you for being the faithful cheerleaders you are.

Thank you to the rest of my family and friends who have been my cheerleaders encouraging me along the way. My gratitude is with my FRWC crew, especially Pastors Jamal Brown and Dr. Paula Brown for being uplifting and pushing me to finish what I started. A few other shout outs are for all the relationships I have been lucky to build at Caron Treatment Center as a whole, my former supervisors, Drs. Maggie Tipton and Michele Pole for allowing the space for me to carve out my focus; my former psychology department that is rock solid in talent and compassion; my Senior VP, Paige Bottom, for your leadership and support; Caron's education and media relations department; and my current team at Caron Outpatient Treatment Center for embracing me (and our very own EMDR certified Clinical Supervisor John Goldman). I cannot leave out my former trauma team for your respect and passionate contributions, dialogue, inspiration, and support; it was truly a pleasure to serve with you. I am grateful for the support I have received during this project from students and faculty at Kutztown University, West Chester University, Alvernia University, and Philadelphia College of Osteopathic Medicine (especially my supporter and friend Dr. Lisa Corbin). And I thank each individual client and patient that has given me the blessing of being a part of their healing journey, that let me in when it was probably one of the scariest things to do.

And without hesitation, I thank my anchor, my God. I may not always know why things happen the way they do, but I do know that I attribute all of who I am today and what I have come through and come to, to you Father God for your grace, your spirit, and your comfort. My faith is the foundation of my perseverance and undeterred nature. With You, I will always RISE. I don't think I can say it better than Lauren Daigle's song *You Say* (2018) "you say I am loved when I can't feel a thing, you say I am strong when I think I am weak, and you say I am held when I am falling short, and when I don't belong, oh you say I am Yours."

About The Author

D r. Ramona Palmerio-Roberts is currently the Executive Director of the Caron Outpatient Treatment Center in Wyomissing, Pa. She is a licensed clinical psychologist and the former Supervisor of Trauma Services for Caron Treatment Centers' main residential campus in Wernersville, Pa. Additionally, Dr. Roberts is a Clinical Associate Professor for the Master's program in counseling at the Philadelphia College of Osteopathic Medicine and teaches both at the undergraduate and graduate level for Alvernia University, West Chester University, and Kutztown University. She is a certified trainer of adolescent co-occurring disorders through the department of health and department of public welfare of Pennsylvania. She received her doctorate degree from Nova Southeastern University in Davie, Florida.

Dr. Roberts is a level II- Certified Clinical Trauma Professional and has trauma trainings that include EMDR, sensorimotor psychotherapy, Internal Family Systems, trauma focused creative art, racialized trauma, and is a Cognitive Processing Therapy provider. She has been interviewed by KYW News radio on Toxic Relationships and WALB Georgia on Racial Trauma. Dr. Roberts has presented to academic and professional audiences at local, regional, national, and intercontinental meetings/ workshops/conferences spanning topics related to trauma; collective trauma; mitigating factors in judicial sentencing;

diversity, equity, inclusion (bias, prejudice, privilege); addiction; and motivational interviewing.

In her earlier role as a full-time faculty member, in addition to teaching, she co-hosted two shows on Neumann Radio on 98.5 WNUW and provided diversity training to Resident Assistants. She has published works in peer-reviewed journals including the *Hispanic Journal of Behavioral Sciences, Journal of Distance Learning and Administration, Academic Exchange Quarterly, Association of Franciscan Colleges and Universities Journal,* and twice in the *National Social Science Journal.*

Dr. Roberts recently received the Inaugural Philadelphia College of Osteopathic Medicine employee diversity, equity, and inclusion award. She has also received awards in the past of Outstanding Club Advisor, Excellence in Undergraduate Teaching, Faculty of the month, and Humanitarian of the Year. She is passionate and focused on being a part of change in creating safe spaces for clients to feel heard, seen, and respected.

References

A.A. Grapevine 12 (1955), p.28

Adelman, Larry. Race: The Power of an Illusion. California Newsreel, 2003.

As/Is. Jose' vs Jose: Who gets a job. YouTube. 8/20/2014. 1:09 min. https://www.youtube.com/watch?v=PR7SG2C7IVU

Baer, R. (2007). *Switching time: A doctor's harrowing story of treating a woman with 17 personalities.* Crown.

Boulware-Brown, P. (2016). *Eagles don't eat chicken food.* Xulan Press.

Brewin, C. R., Kleiner, J. S., Vasterling, J. J., & Field, A. P. (2007). Memory for emotionally neutral information in posttraumatic stress disorder: A meta-analytic investigation. *Journal of Abnormal Psychology,* 116, 448-463.

Brickel, Robyn. "How people cope with trauma they want to forget," March 6, 2020, https://brickelandassociates.com/dissociation-from-trauma/

Brickel, Robyn. "Using 'Big T' and 'Little T' for Trauma Can Be a Big Mistake," May 9, 2019, https://brickelandassociates.com/big-t-little-t-trauma/

Briggs-Gowan, M. J., Ford, J. D., Fraleigh, L., McCarthy, K., & Carter, A. S. (2010). Prevalence of exposure to potentially traumatic events in a healthy birth cohort of very young children in the northeastern United States. Journal of Traumatic Stress, 23, 725–733.

Broderick, P. & Blewitt, P. (2020). *The life span: Human development for helping professionals* (5th ed.). New York: Pearson.

Buchanan, T. W. (2007). Retrieval of emotional memories. *Psychological Bulletin*, 133, 761-779.

Carter, R. T. (2007). Racism and Psychological and Emotional Injury: Recognizing and Assessing Race-Based Traumatic Stress. *The Counseling Psychologist*, *35*(1), 13–105.

Cloitre, M. (2020). ICD-11 complex post-traumatic stress disorder: Simplifying diagnosis in trauma populations. *The British Journal of Psychiatry*, 216(3), 129-131.

Daigle, L. (2018). *You Say*. Centricity Warner Bros.

Damasio, A., & Carvalho, G. B. (2013). The nature of feelings: Evolutionary and neurobiological origins. *Nature Reviews/Neuroscience*, 14, 143-152.

Damasio, A.R. (1994). *Descartes' error: Emotion, reason, and the human brain*. New York, NY: Grosset/Putnam

Ecker, B., Ticic, R., & Hulley, L. (2012). *Unlocking the emotional brain: Eliminating symptoms at their roots using memory reconsolidation.* Routledge.

Elkind, D. (1967). Egocentrism in adolescence. *Child Development,* 38 (4), 1025-1034.

Extremera, N., & Rey, L. (2016). Ability emotional intelligence and life satisfaction: Positive and negative affect as mediators. *Personality and Individual differences, 102,* 98-101.

Felitti, V. J., Anda, R. F., Nordenberg, D., Williamson, D. F., Spitz, A. M., Edwards, V., Koss, M. P., & Marks, J. S. (1998). Relationship of childhood abuse and household dysfunction to many of the leading causes of death in adults: The Adverse Childhood Experiences (ACE) Study. *American Journal of Preventive Medicine, 14*(4), 245–258.

Feinstein, J. S., Duff, M. C., & Tranel, D. (2010). Sustained experiences of emotion after loss of memory in patients with amnesia. *Proceedings of the National Academy of Sciences,* 107, 7674-7679.

Fisher, Janina. (2017). Clinical Trauma Professional Training Level 1 Working with the neurobiological legacy of trauma.

Forbes, H. (2017). Understanding the conversation behind the behavior. North American Council on Adoptable Children.

Fusion Comedy. How microaggressions are like mosquito bites-same difference. YouTube. 10/5/2016. 1:57 min. https://www.youtube.com/watch?v=hDd3bzA7450

Hardy, K. (2015). How to talk effectively about race. https://aims.uw.edu/nyscc/training/sites/default/files/Talk%20About%20Race.pdf

Harlow, H. F., Harlow, M. L., & Suomi, S. J. (1971). From thought to therapy: Lessons from a primate laboratory. *American Scientist, 59*, 538-549.

Harvey, M. (1990). An ecological view of psychological trauma and recovery from trauma. In *meeting of the International Society of Traumatic Stress Studies, New Orleans, LA*.

Integrative Psychiatry Institute. Yehuda, R. Intergenerational transmission of trauma. 4/5/2021. 4:52 min. https://www.youtube.com/watch?v=8Qfrcjck3vY&t=1s

Izard, C. E. (2009). Emotion theory and research: Highlights, unanswered questions, and emerging issues. *Annual Review of Psychology, 60*, 1-25.

Kenzinger, E. A. (2007). Negative emotion enhances memory accuracy: Behavioral and neuroimaging evidence. *Current Directions in Psychological Science*, 16, 213-218.

Lerner, M. J. (1980). The belief in a just world. In *The Belief in a just World* (pp. 9-30). Springer, Boston, MA.

Mary J. Blige., & Mary J. Blige|ARTIST. (2007). *Growing Pains*. Geffen Records.

McDonough, C., Palmerio-Roberts, R., & de Gordon, M. T. (2020). What's in a name? What attributions do you make about people with names like Jennifer, D'Shaun, Martinez and Chen?. *National social science journal, 55*(1), 14-22.

McGaugh, J. L. (2003). *Memory and emotion: The making of lasting memories.* New York: Columbia University Press.

Meyers, D.G. (2014) *Exploring Psychology.* 9th Ed. Worth Publishers, NY. New York

National Alliance For The Mentally Ill, U. S. (2022) National Alliance on Mental Illness NAMI. United States. [Web Archive] Retrieved from the Library of Congress, https://www.loc.gov/item/lcwaN0000280/.

Ogden, P., Minton, K., & Pain, C. (2006). *Trauma and the body: A sensorimotor approach to psychotherapy.* W. W. Norton & Company.

Oxnam, R. (2005). *A Fractured Mind: My life with multiple personality disorder.* Hyperion.

Pettigrew, T. F. (1979). The ultimate attribution error: Extending Allport's cognitive analysis of prejudice. *Personality and Social Psychology Bulletin,* 55, 461-476.

Rajmohan, V., & Mohandas, E. (2007). The limbic system. *Indian journal of psychiatry, 49*(2), 132–139

Ross, L. (1977). The intuitive psychologist and his shortcomings: Distortions in the attribution process. In L. Berkowitz (Ed.), *Advances in experimental social psychology* (Vol. 10, pp. 174-221). New York, NY: Academic Press.

Salovey, P., & Mayer, J. D. (1990) Emotional intelligence. *Imagination, Cognition, and Personality,* 9, 185-211.

Siegel, D.J. (1999). *The developing mind: toward a neurobiology of interpersonal experience.* New York: Guilford Press

Silverbush, L., et. al. (2013). *A Place at the Table*. Magnolia Pictures.

Skinner, B. F. (1938). Behavior of organisms. New York: Appleton-Century-Crofts.

Spring, C. (2016). *Recovery is my best revenge: My experience of trauma, abuse and dissociative identity disorder*. Pods Trauma Training Ltd.

Spring, C. (2019). *Unshame: Healing trauma-based shame through psychotherapy*. Pods Trauma Training Ltd.

Sue, D. W., & Sue, D. (2019). *Counseling the culturally diverse: Theory and practice* (8th ed). Hoboken, New Jersey: John Wiley & Sons, Inc.

Tedeschi R. G. (2020). Growth after trauma. *Harvard Business Review: Crisis Management*. July-August.

Tedeschi R. G., & Calhoun L. G. (1996). The Posttraumatic Growth Inventory: measuring the positive legacy of trauma. J Trauma Stress. Jul;9(3):455-71.

Tatum, B. D. (2017). *Why are all the black kids sitting together in the cafeteria?* Basic Books/Hachette Book Group.

van der Kolk, B. (2014). *The body keeps the score: Brain, mind, and body in the healing of trauma*. Viking.

Wang G, Zhang Y, Zhao J, Zhang J, Jiang F. (2020). Mitigate the effects of home confinement on children during the COVID-19 outbreak. *Lancet*, 395, 945-947.

Walker, L. NSU College of Psychology. (2020). *Intimate partner relationships in times of crisis*. [webinar]. https://www.youtube.com/watch?v=LXitz8msZE0

Walker, Tim. "How 'Zoom Fatigue' impacts communication with students." National Education Association. 10/16/2020. https://www.nea.org/advocating-for-change/new-from-nea/how-zoom-fatigue-impacts-communication-students

World Health Organization. (2019). *ICD-11: International classification of diseases* (11th revision). Retrieved from https://icd.who.int/